P9-ELX-686

Tales Alive!

Books by Susan Milord

Adventures in Art:
Art & Craft Experiences for 7- to 14-Year-Olds

Hands Around the World:
365 Creative Ways to Build Cultural Awareness
and Global Respect

The Kids' Nature Book:
365 Indoor/Outdoor Activities and Experiences

Tales Alive! Ten Multicultural Folktales
With Activities

Tales Alive!

TEN MULTICULTURAL FOLKTALES WITH ACTIVITIES

as retold by
SUSAN MILORD

Paintings by
MICHAEL A. DONATO

WILLIAMSON PUBLISHING
CHARLOTTE, VERMONT

Copyright © 1995 by Susan Milord

All rights reserved.

No portion of this book may be reproduced–mechanically, electronically, or by any other means, including photocopying–without written permission of the publisher.

Library of Congress Cataloging-in-Publication Data

Milord, Susan.
    Tales alive!: ten multicultural folktales with
    activities/by Susan Milord.
            p.   cm.
    Includes index.
    ISBN 0-913589-79-9
    1. Tales. 2. Multiculturalism--Juvenile literature.
    3. Creative activities and seat work--Juvenile literature.
    [1.Folklore. 2. Amusements.] I. Title
GR69.M55   1994
398.2--dc20   94-101
                                     CIP
                                     AC

Design by JOSEPH LEE
Paintings by MICHAEL A. DONATO
Activity illustrations by MICHAEL KLINE, ACME DESIGN CO.
Printed by IMAGO SALES (USA), INC.
Printed in CHINA

WILLIAMSON PUBLISHING
P. O. Box 185
Charlotte, VT 05445
Telephone: (800) 234-8791
10 9 8 7 6 5 4 3 2 1

Dedicated to the world's storytellers, who keep the tales alive.

This book was made possible by the support, encouragement, and creativity of many people. My heartfelt thanks go to Jack and Susan Williamson, who made a dream come true. Many thanks to Bill Jaspersohn, who edited my words with utmost care, and became a friend in the process. I can't thank Joseph Lee enough for designing such a gorgeous book, made even more wonderful thanks to Michael A. Donato's sublime paintings. Thanks, also, to Michael Kline and John Baxter of Acme Design, who provided many of the illustrations that accompany the activities. All of you did what I could not have done alone: you have truly infused the tales—and this book—with life.

Permission was granted to use the following primary source material:

"The Tale of the Gentle Folk" by Charles J. Finger, from *Tales from Silver Lands* (Doubleday & Company, 1924).

"A Drum" by A.K. Ramanujan, from *Folktales from India* (Pantheon Books, 1991).

"Why the Hare Runs Away" retold by Roger D. Abrahams, from *African Folktales* (Pantheon Books, 1983).

"The Story of Campriano" by Italo Calvino, from *Italian Folktales* (Harcourt Brace and Company, 1980).

"The Beekeeper and the Bewitched Hare" by Sorche Nic Leodhas, from *Thistle & Thyme: Tales and Legends from Scotland* (Holt, Rinehart and Winston, 1962). Copyright © 1962 by Leclaire G. Alger. Copyright © 1990 by Louis R. Hoffman.

"The Morning Star: The Barnumbir Myth" by Louis A. Allen, from *Time Before Morning* (Thomas Y. Crowell, 1975).

"Urashima the Fisherman" edited and translated by Royall Tyler, from *Japanese Tales* (Pantheon Books, 1987).

"A Mirror, a Carpet, and a Lemon" by Barbara K. Walker, from *A Treasury of Turkish Folktales for Children* (Linnet Books, 1988). Copyright © 1988 Barbara K. Walker.

Additional sources can be found on pages 124-125.

Notice: the information contained in this book is complete and accurate to the best of our knowledge. All recommendations and suggestions are made without any guarantees on the part of the author or Williamson Publishing. The author and publisher disclaim all liability incurred in connection with the use of this information.

Contents

✗

Once Upon a Time . . .   8

Tales and Activities

Once Upon a Time . . .

✗

 torytelling is a heritage the whole world shares, and *Tales Alive!* is a collection of ten wonderful stories taken from that rich heritage. From the fabled reaches of czarist Russia to the coastal regions down under in Australia, here are some of the timeless tales enjoyed by people around the globe.

In this book you'll find legends that explain the creation of the natural world, tales about tricksters, parables about people who are turned into animals, and about animals that turn—you guessed it!—into people. There are tales that will make you laugh out loud, tales that will have you on the edge of your seat, and tales that will make you scratch your head in wonder.

This book is more than just a sampling of tales, however. Each story in *Tales Alive!* is followed by activities that help explain the story and bring it to life. The activities are inspired by the stories themselves and their characters, as well as by the cultures from which the stories come.

As you read these stories and do the activities, you'll learn something about the different types of tales people tell. You'll be able to compare some of the ways storytellers prepare their listeners for a journey to the land of make-believe. You'll get the chance to retell these stories in other ways, such as in rhyming verse and various types of art. You'll dine on delicious foods inspired by the stories, and you'll create beautiful crafts that you can wear or use in your home. And there's plenty of additional hands-on fun, from simple science experiments to age-old games to riddles, puzzles, and brainteasers.

So, come along on this journey to faraway places and long-ago times and meet the clever heroes, fierce fighters, and merry madcaps who make these tales so special. Then use the activities to further bring these characters and their stories to life. Tales alive!

TRULY TALES OF THE WORLD

The ten tales in this book come from all over the world, each from a different country. Some of the stories may sound familiar, and you may even have heard similar stories from other countries. That's not surprising. Some tales are told in many different places, even continents apart. There may be slight differences in the details, but the basic story is the same.

For example, one of the stories in this collection, "The Clever Maiden," from Russia, resembles tales from other countries. Perhaps you know one of the Italian versions (in one, the maiden is named Catherine). Or you might have heard the popular retelling from Slovakia, where the girl is known as Manka. Tales of clever peasant girls abound in these and other countries throughout the world. The same is true of many of the other tales in this collection.

What does this tell us? That folktales are just another of the many things the world's people have in common with each other.

BRINGING THE TALES TO LIFE

Doing the activities that follow each tale is as much fun as reading the stories themselves. You'll find plenty to interest you, and all the projects are easy enough for you to do on your own, with minimal help from an adult. (Of course, the grown-ups may want to get in on some of the fun!) To fully enjoy the activities, keep the following in mind:

◉ *Be sure to first read through an activity from start to finish before beginning it. That way, you'll know what to expect, see what materials you'll need, and have a clear understanding of the step-by-step instructions. Ask grown-ups for help if you have any questions. They can also help you round up supplies or suggest substitutions for materials you may not have on hand.*

◉ *There are times you should have adult supervision, such as when cooking at the stove or handling a sharp tool. Whenever an adult's help is required for an activity, you will be reminded to ask for it before going on to the next step.*

◉ *Most of the projects in this book take less than an hour to complete, some much less than an hour. (A few take longer—mostly to allow papier-mâché and paint to dry completely.) Don't worry if you aren't sure if you have enough time to complete a project. Many projects have convenient stopping points. Check the instructions to see where you might be able to leave your work and come back to it later.*

◉ *Have fun!*

A WORD TO ADULTS

Tales Alive! is a book meant to appeal to children in a wide range of ages—there's a little something for everyone. While the text is written directly to children—and older kids can certainly read the stories and do many of the projects on their own—this is also a book that children and adults can enjoy together. After all, younger children aren't the only ones who enjoy listening to stories read aloud, and sharing activities like those that follow each tale is a great way for families to spend time together.

The ten tales in this collection offer lots of inspiration, but think of them and the accompanying activities as jumping-off places. You and the children will no doubt come up with plenty of other ideas to bring these stories to life—from cooking an entire meal from one of the countries mentioned to learning about the customs, languages, and history of those regions. Use your interest and knowledge of other cultures to extend your "visits" to the various countries touched upon in this book. The tales will be all the richer for it, as will the time you spend with your kids.

Finally, teachers, day-care providers, and youth-group leaders will also find enjoyment using *Tales Alive!* with your students. As you'll see, the questions posed in the activities sections lend themselves to group discussion, and the hands-on projects can be adapted to larger groups of kids.

✗

This tale from Patagonia, a region in the southernmost part of
South America, describes how a peaceful group of people are forced to
make a difficult decision in order to save their way of life.

The Gentle People

ong, long ago this land was home to a community of gentle people who were as happy and content as they could be. They lived in complete harmony with one another and with all the natural world.

Theirs was a beautiful land, crisscrossed by clear streams and brightened by sparkling jewels that lay upon the ground. The countryside was blanketed with sweet-smelling flowers, because when one was picked, two more grew in its place. The people had a special magic to turn flowers into living birds, and so the air was filled with happy birdsong from morning till night. And all the wild animals, even the shyest creatures, were fearless and tame.

The gentle folk were ruled by a kindly prince who was as wise as he was good. He gathered his people together on the eve of each full moon to celebrate the community's good fortune. The animals and birds would join them, sharing in the music and laughter. Once a year a special celebration was held, and on this day each person was granted one wish. Life was so good that the gentle people often could think of nothing to wish for.

There was one thing the prince forbade the people to do, and that was to journey so far north that they no longer could see the stars of the Southern Cross.

The prince told his people that a forest stood just beyond that point, a forest so dense that daylight never penetrated it.

As none of the people had any wish to leave their own country, nor any desire to visit this forbidden place, they were not troubled by their prince's warning.

One day a member of the community chanced upon a bird unlike any he had seen before. Its shimmering feathers were colored like the rainbow, and its song was so haunting that it stopped the man in his tracks. The man drew closer to the bird to see it more clearly, but when he was near enough to touch it, the bird flitted away to another branch.

The man was puzzled because no bird in this happy land had ever done that before. He tried to approach it again, speaking soothingly and extending his hand. The bird flew a short distance away, to another tree.

The man was completely enchanted by this mysterious bird, and followed after it. The bird fluttered from one tree to another, and before he knew what had happened, the man found that he'd been led right into the forbidden forest. It was so dark that he could not even see his hand in front of his face.

The man blindly stumbled on until he found himself in a small clearing where a group of fierce-looking men were gathered around a fire. They were clothed in ragged skins, and their teeth were yellow and pointed. Some were eating the raw flesh of animals; others were arguing and roughly shoving one another.

When the fierce ones spied the man from the gentle people, they quickly surrounded him, tearing at his clothing. Some grabbed the feathers from his hair; others snatched the gems he wore on his fingers and around his neck and wrists. The man was even more astounded when the brutes began fighting among themselves for the things they had taken from him. Horrified, he turned and ran from the forest, not stopping until he was back among his own people.

The man went straight to the prince to tell him what he had seen in the dark woods. The prince listened to his tale in silence. "You have met the greedy and selfish people," he said with a grave voice. "I hoped this day would never come. I must call a gathering of our people to let them know what has happened and to decide what we must do."

And so a meeting was called. All the people, animals, and birds gathered as they always did at celebration time, filling the air with laughter and song. But when they saw the sad face of their prince, they fell silent and waited for him to speak.

"I have terrible news for you all," the prince began. "The greedy and selfish people who live in the dark forest have discovered us." Then the prince asked the man to tell the others what he had seen in that cheerless place. For the first time, the gentle people could not smile but looked at each other sadly.

"The selfish ones will not be satisfied until they have discovered where we live," the prince told his people. "We must prepare ourselves for their arrival."

"How will we do that?" asked a woman in the crowd.

"If you like, I can arm you all with weapons, and we can fight the greedy ones when they come," the prince said. He paused for a moment, then continued. "But you'll be taking a great risk if you do that. Having learned to fight and to kill and bring death upon others, you will turn upon each other and bring death to your own people. The animals will learn to fear you and will run from you when they hear you approaching. The flowers will no longer blossom as they do now, and the sparkling gems will be hidden from sight deep within the earth."

The people all looked at one another, shaking their heads.

"We do not want that to happen," they said. "Is there no way we can change our shape so the greedy ones do not recognize us?"

The prince thought for a moment. "Follow me!" he urged his people, turning and running. The gentle people hurried after him, and not a moment too soon, because the greedy and selfish people had just crested a nearby hill, trampling flowers and kicking up stones as they came.

The people ran, and when they reached the river, the prince told them they would be changed once they had crossed to the other side. The people splashed into the shallows, and, one by one, as they climbed up on the far shore, they turned into guanacos (hwa-NAH-cohs), relatives of the gentle llama. The prince was the last to ford the river, and he, too, was transformed into a guanaco, slightly larger than the rest.

To this day, when you see these stately creatures gathered in their herds, you can always tell which one is the prince. He is the tallest one, standing guard away from the others. He is keeping a lookout for the greedy and selfish people.

It is said that whenever a guanaco dies, a gold-tipped blue flower springs up in its place. When the very last guanaco left on earth finally dies, the greedy and selfish people will also be extinct. When that happens, the blue flowers will all bend their heads to the earth together, and the gentle people will return to their land, to live in harmony with the natural world, as they once did, long ago.

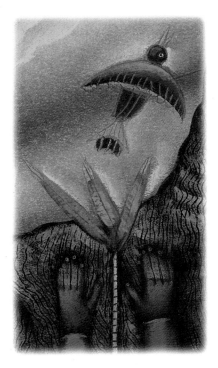

THE
GENTLE
PEOPLE

WHERE IN THE WORLD IS ARGENTINA?

COUNTRY:	**Argentina**
CONTINENT:	**South America**
LANGUAGE:	**Spanish**
CAPITAL:	**Buenos Aires**
FLAG:	

WISHFUL THINKING

Life was so good for the gentle people in this story that they rarely wished for anything because there was little they wanted that they didn't already have.

If only things were that way today! Unhappily, people throughout the world must cope with many problems, from hunger to homelessness to the fear of violence and outright war. The natural world, too, is endangered. Plants and animals all over the globe are struggling to survive as the wild places on earth steadily shrink.

What would you like to see different about the world, not only where you live but in other places, too? If you were granted one wish that could change things for the better, what would you wish for?

Ask your family and friends this same question and make a "wish list" of everyone's responses. Then see if there is anything you can do—no matter how small—to help one of these wishes come true.

Wish List

Person:	Wish:
Ramona	a steady job for my Dad
Elise	a great school year
Jason	get my braces off early
Mom	an end to hunger in the world
Peter	good health
Jamal	straight A's this ter...

camel

guanaco

GENTLE BEASTS

In "The Gentle People" the prince and his people are turned into guanacos to save themselves from the selfish and greedy people. Had you ever heard of the guanaco before you read this tale?

Even if you hadn't, you probably are familiar with another South American animal closely related to the guanaco—the llama (YAH-mah). In fact, some people say the guanaco and the llama are identical, only the guanaco remains a wild animal, while the llama was domesticated by people hundreds of years ago.

Guanacos and llamas (and their close cousins the alpaca and vicuña) are also related to the camel, which lives halfway across the world in Africa. Can you see the family resemblance?

The guanaco, like the camel, has successfully adapted to life in a harsh climate. High in the mountains where guanacos live, there is less oxygen and the climate is very cold. Lack of oxygen doesn't seem to bother this sturdy beast, and its thick, woolly coat protects it from the cold.

THE STARS ABOVE DOWN BELOW

The one thing the gentle people are warned they must never do is travel so far north that they can no longer see the stars of the *Southern Cross.* If you have never heard of this constellation—a group of stars that has been given a name—it's probably because you don't live where it can be seen.

You may be familiar with some of the constellations that are visible in the night sky where you live, such as the *Big Dipper* and the *Little Dipper.*

The Southern Cross is just as famous as the two Dippers, at least to people who live in the *Southern Hemisphere* (south of the Equator).

The Southern Cross is a small constellation, but its distinctive cross shape makes it easy to spot. It is also visible all year long, in much the same location in the sky (directly overhead). If you didn't know this cluster of four stars was called the Southern Cross, what name might you give it?

SCENT-SATIONAL FLOWERS

Did you know that some of the sweetest-smelling flowers commonly grown in gardens came originally from South America? Maybe some of these are descended from the magical flowers in "The Gentle People"!

You can easily grow some of these flowers, even if you don't have a garden. Most grow well in pots. All you need is a spot that gets lots of sun each day. The plants listed here are all *perennials* (plants that grow year after year) in warmer climates, but many gardeners grow them as *annuals* (plants that live for just one summer).

Check your local gardening center in the spring for plants all ready to put into the ground (or containers) once it is warm enough where you live. Or start your own plants from seed. All you need is a sunny window, a paper milk carton sliced in half lengthwise and punched with drainage holes, and purchased potting soil (be sure to dampen the soil thoroughly before putting it into the carton halves).

Follow the planting instructions on the seed packets and check for the best time to sow the seeds. This chart lists a few varieties you'll want to try.

FLOWER NAME	HEIGHT	COLOR	WHEN TO SOW
heliotrope	15-24 inches (37-60 cm)	blue, violet, and white	Sow indoors 8 weeks before consistently warm weather. Plant is very sensitive to cold.
nasturtium (Not a particularly fragrant plant, but a lovely one. The flowers are edible. Toss some in a salad!)	8-24 inches (20-60 cm) Some varieties are climbing plants.	rose to yellow to orange to maroon	Sow directly in the ground, as the plants do not react well to transplanting.
nicotiana (also known as flowering tobacco)	10-30 inches (25-75 cm)	white, red, pink, and lavender	Sow indoors 4 to 6 weeks before last spring frost (may take several weeks to come up).
verbena	8-10 inches (20-25 cm)	white, lavender, pink, and red	Sow indoors 12 weeks before last spring frost.

NATURE'S BOUNTY

The gentle people stuck brightly colored feathers in their hair and wore rings, bracelets, and necklaces made from precious gems.

Here is a necklace the gentle people would surely have loved, only this one is made of paper and a lightweight string called embroidery floss. This necklace has plenty of "feathers" and glittering "gemstone" beads. String one up for yourself or make some to give as gifts.

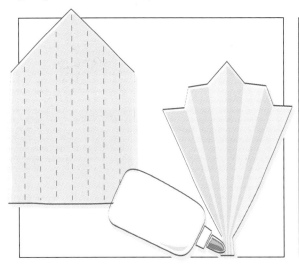

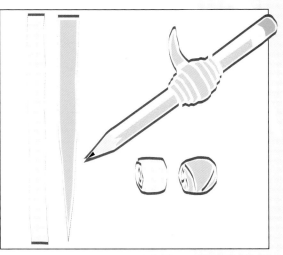

1 To make "feathers," cut five-sided shapes from heavy paper. Fold each shape accordion-style, creasing the folds well. Squirt some glue between the folds at the end that is not pointed. Pinch the folds together and hold for a few seconds until the paper has bonded.

2 To make "gemstone" beads, cut ¼-inch to ½-inch (.6 cm to 1.2 cm) strips of shiny paper. Taper some of the strips to make barrel-shaped beads. The strip lengths will depend on the thickness of paper (the thinner the paper, the longer the strip needs to be to make a sturdy bead). Place a tiny bit of glue on one end of each strip and wrap tightly around a pencil or knitting needle. Glue the end of the strip, then slip the bead off the pencil.

YOU'LL NEED

- ○ **Assorted paper, including heavyweight colored paper and metallic paper (such as gift wrap)**
- ○ **Scissors**
- ○ **Pencil**
- ○ **White glue**
- ○ **Embroidery floss**
- ○ **Large, blunt needle**

3 Carefully poke holes through the pinched ends of the "feathers" with the needle. Thread the needle with the embroidery floss and string the necklace, placing "gemstone" beads between the "feathers" to separate them. Knot the end of the floss and try the necklace on!

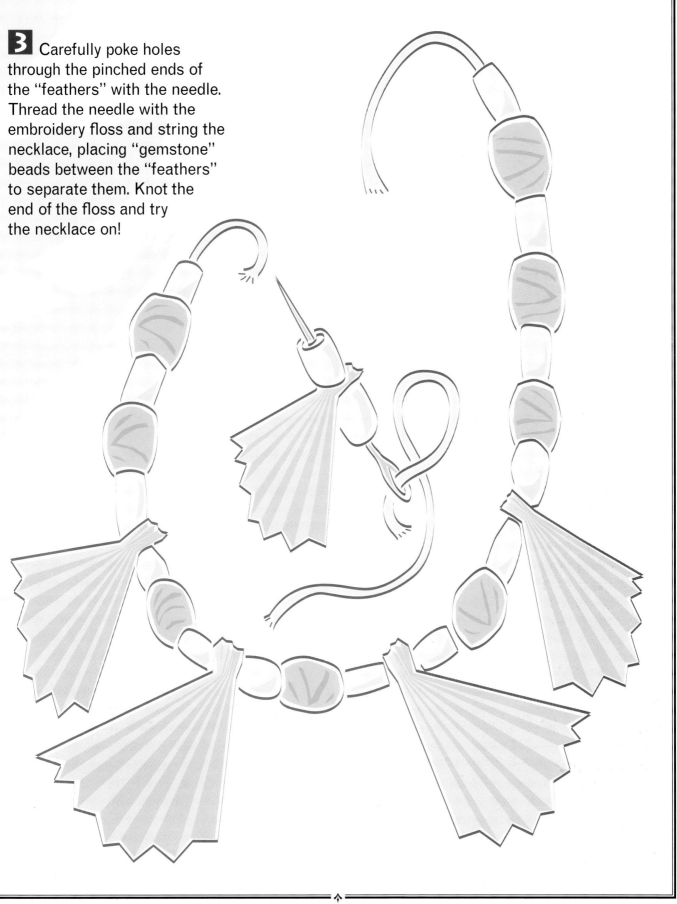

There are many different versions of this Russian tale told throughout the world. In each, a peasant girl impresses a man of importance (sometimes a tax collector, a mayor of a town, or a king) with her responses to the questions she is asked or the tasks that she is given.

The Clever Maiden

Once upon a time there lived a farmer who was so poor he didn't have enough money to pay his taxes one year. He planned on giving the czar, the powerful ruler of the land, just a small portion of what he owed now and paying the rest later. The farmer had often done this before, but his daughter said, "I don't think that will work this year, Father. I am sure the czar will want nothing less than the full amount."

When the czar arrived at the farmer's cottage to collect the tax money, he was angered that the farmer did not have all the money. "You must pay all that is due," the czar declared, "and nothing less."

The farmer hung his head. "I should have listened to my daughter," he said. "She was certain that you would accept nothing less than all the money this year."

"Is your daughter really that clever?" asked the czar.

"She is," the maiden's father replied.

"I'll tell you what I'll do, then," the czar said. "Don't worry about the taxes for now. Tomorrow I will send over a basketful of eggs that need hatching. I, myself, will return in a week's time to collect the chicks. But if your daughter does not succeed in hatching them," he warned with a stern look, "I shall have no choice but to throw you both in prison."

The eggs arrived the next day, and the maiden examined them carefully.

She held them in her hands and weighed them, and then saw to her dismay that the eggs were all hard-boiled.

"Oh, no!" wailed the farmer. "Now we shall be thrown in prison for sure."

"Don't worry, father," the maiden replied. "It won't come to that. I'll think of something."

Well, the morning the czar was expected to pick up the chicks, the maiden boiled up a handful of dried beans. She gave them to her father and told him to work in the garden alongside the lane to their cottage. "When the czar is within earshot," the maiden went on, "be sure to call out, 'May these boiled beans grow stout and tall!'"

The farmer did as his daughter had instructed him, and as she predicted, the czar stopped his carriage, shaking his head in disbelief. "Foolish man," he cried out, "how can you think those boiled beans will ever grow?"

Recalling what his daughter had told him to say, the farmer replied, "The same way chicks will hatch from boiled eggs!" Seeing that the

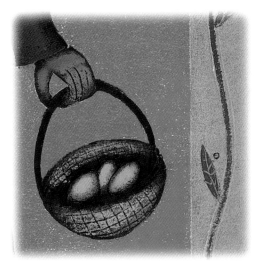

maiden had not fallen for his trick, the czar threw back his head and laughed, and ordered his carriage home.

The czar was a proud man, however, and his game wasn't over yet. A week later he brought a skein of yarn to the farmer's home and ordered the maiden to weave enough cloth to clothe all his palace servants. . . or else. The farmer wrung his hands with worry, but the maiden took it all very calmly. "Don't fret, father," she said. "I'll think of something."

When the czar returned for the cloth, the maiden handed him a piece of wood. "I'll weave the cloth once you have made me a loom from this single piece of wood," she said. Once again, the czar was enchanted by the maiden's clever answer.

The czar paid a third visit to the cottage, this time with a tiny silver cup in hand. "Maiden, with this cup I would like you to empty the seas surrounding my palace so that I may have more pastureland for my animals."

The following week he smiled when the maiden presented him with a smooth stone. "I shall empty the seas surrounding your palace when you are able to block up all the rivers of the world with this one stone," she said.

The czar was not really a heartless man, despite his position of power. From his weekly visits, he had grown to love the farmer's daughter. For her part, the maiden had also fallen in love with this man who valued her cleverness. The farmer was very pleased—and relieved!—when the czar announced that he wished to marry the maiden.

What a grand wedding it was, followed by a fabulous feast and dancing until dawn. Before the tired and happy couple went to bed, the maiden—or czarina, as she would now be called—took her husband aside and placed a piece of parchment and a pen in his hand.

"I ask just one small favor of you," she said. "Please put in writing that, if you are ever displeased with me and ask me to leave my new home, I be allowed to take with me any one thing that I treasure above all else."

The czar agreed to this request and wrote out the words. He signed his name to the document, then folded it and sealed it with sealing wax pressed flat with his royal ring.

Several years passed, and they were happy ones, but as married couples do everywhere, the czar and czarina quarreled one evening. In his anger, the czar shouted, "Woman, you are impossible! Get out of my sight! I wish never to see you again!"

"As you please," the czarina replied. "But it's late. I will pack my belongings now, but allow me to leave in the morning."

The czar grudgingly agreed. He took his usual bedtime drink upstairs to the bed chamber, unaware that his wife had slipped a sleeping potion into the cup. When he was sound asleep, the czarina ordered that the royal carriage be readied and the czar put into it. The snoring ruler slept throughout the journey to the cottage where the maiden had once lived with her father.

When the czar awoke the next morning, he rose up in bed and looked around him. "Where am I, and who holds me here?" he demanded.

"I hold you here, dear husband," answered the czarina, entering the room. "And I hold in my hand the parchment you penned on our wedding night. May I remind you of what it says? You agreed that if ever I were to leave the palace I might take with me that which I treasured most."

"I recall your request well," the czar laughed. "And I am honored by your love. I spoke without thinking yesterday, and I apologize for my harsh words. I treasure you above all else, too."

So saying, the czar kissed his wife, and they returned to the palace, where they lived happily for many more years.

COUNTRY: **Russia**
CONTINENT: **Europe, Asia**
LANGUAGE: **Russian**
CAPITAL: **Moscow**
FLAG:

Answer: Man, who crawls on the ground on all fours when an infant, walks upright on two feet in the middle of life, and uses a cane—a third leg—in old age.

ANSWER ME THIS

Successfully solving a puzzle of some sort is a feature of many folktales, not just those about clever peasant girls. In some stories, the hero or heroine must answer a riddle. And as you know, riddles aren't always what they seem!

Many very old riddles continue to puzzle people today, including this ancient Greek puzzler that is known as "the riddle of the Sphinx." See if you can solve it. (Check the margin if you're stumped.)

What moves on four feet in the morning, two feet at noon, and three feet in the evening?

Some riddles are not asked as questions but are puzzling statements, like the examples from three different countries shown here. All of these riddles have the same answer. Can you guess what it is?

   Try these riddles on your family or your friends. Is anyone able to come up with the answers?

A horse with a silver tail neighs on a high hill.
—*Lithuania*

Round as a hoop, deep as a pail;
Never sings out till it's caught by the tail.
—*Newfoundland*

Señora Carolina lives in a high house, and when they pull her feet, she wakes up all the townspeople.
—*Chile*

Answer to all three riddles: A bell in a bell tower. If you were to invent your own riddle with this answer, how would it go?

THREE, COUNT 'EM, THREE!

The czar visits the maiden three times, giving her three tasks to perform. Three is a number you'll find in many tales. Just think of the three little pigs, and the three wishes the genie grants Aladdin. What's so special about the number three?

In this story at least, the maiden was given three tests to be sure she just wasn't lucky. After all, if something happens once, you don't think anything of it; if it happens twice, you begin to wonder; and if it happens a third time, there must be something to it!

Here's a puzzle (based on the number three, of course!) that might have stumped even the clever maiden. We've chosen beans for this puzzle, in honor of the boiled beans in the story, but you can use pebbles, coins, or other counters. Don't worry if you can't come up with the solution right away—or at all. See the solution at the edge of the page.

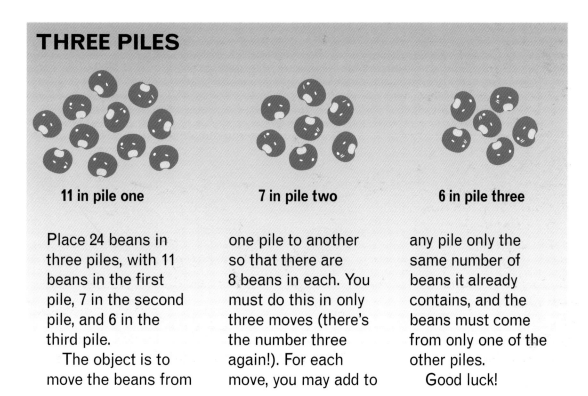

THREE PILES

11 in pile one

7 in pile two

6 in pile three

Place 24 beans in three piles, with 11 beans in the first pile, 7 in the second pile, and 6 in the third pile.

The object is to move the beans from one pile to another so that there are 8 beans in each. You must do this in only three moves (there's the number three again!). For each move, you may add to any pile only the same number of beans it already contains, and the beans must come from only one of the other piles.

Good luck!

Solution: Move seven beans from pile 1 to pile 2; move six beans from pile 2 to pile 3; move four beans from pile 3 to pile 1.

COLD COMFORT

Having lived all her life in a small cottage, it probably took some time for the maiden to get used to the size of the czar's palace. She may even have gotten lost a few times as she wandered through the vast rooms and corridors!

You can build your own miniature version of a rambling palace, complete with cone-topped towers and crenellated walls. You need freezing weather or a freezer compartment for this project, however, because this royal abode is made completely of ice.

Lots of containers in various sizes and shapes, such as empty milk cartons, frozen juice cans, shoe boxes lined with plastic wrap, plastic bowls, yogurt and cottage cheese containers, ice cube trays

1 Find a level place outdoors or a big enough space in your family's freezer for your assortment of containers. Fill the containers with water and leave them overnight to freeze.

2 The next day, remove the frozen blocks of ice by dipping the containers into a large bowl of warm water just long enough so that the ice slips out of the containers.

Build a palace using all the ice shapes, holding the pieces together with a little water splashed onto the surfaces you wish to join. If you are building your palace outdoors, be careful not to touch your wet fingers to cold metal. Bring a towel with you to dry your hands.

Be sure to take a photograph of your ice palace, because once the sun comes out and warms the air, it won't be there for long!

EGG-CEPTIONAL EGGS

Eggs certainly played an important role in this story. After all, if the maiden hadn't figured out what to do with the hard-boiled eggs she was given to hatch, the story might have ended right there.

When many people think of Russia and eggs, the famous Imperial Easter eggs come to mind. More than 50 of them were made from 1886 to 1916. The first was a gift from Czar Alexander III to his wife, Maria, in 1886. It was crafted in the studio of a clever jeweler named Peter Carl Fabergé. Made entirely of gold, the egg looked just like a real hen's egg from the outside. But the shell opened to reveal a tiny hen with ruby eyes, nesting on a bed of gold straw!

You can make your own "jeweled" egg for Easter—or any other time of year. Like the first Fabergé egg, this one opens up to hold tiny treasures or trinkets.

YOU'LL NEED

○ **Non-hardening modeling clay, about 8 ounces (250 g)**
○ **Petroleum jelly**
○ **Newspaper, torn in ½-inch (1.2 cm) strips**
○ **Papier-mâché paste, made from 2 cups (250 g) flour mixed with 2 cups (500 ml) water until smooth**
○ **Serrated kitchen knife**
○ **Sandpaper**
○ **Acrylic paints**
○ **Paintbrush**
○ **Assorted trims, such as sequins, beads, and shiny ribbon**
○ **White glue**
○ **Thin, white cardboard**

1 Shape the clay into an egg shape. Cover the egg completely with petroleum jelly. With the papier-mâché mixture, paste at least eight layers of overlapping newspaper strips over the clay egg. Set the egg in a warm place for several days until it is completely dry.

2 Have an adult cut the egg in half with the serrated knife. "Sawing" through the papier-mâché and the clay requires care and strength. Remove the clay from each half of the egg (it can be reused, so don't throw it away).

3 Sand the outside of the shells; then paint the shells both inside and out, with two coats if needed.

4 Now to make your egg really sparkle, glue an assortment of sequins, faceted beads, and cloth trims to the outside of the shells. Let dry.

5 Measure around the inside of one of the egg halves. Cut a 1/2-inch-wide (1.2 cm) strip of thin cardboard that length. Glue the cardboard strip to the inside of one shell half, letting the strip extend slightly above the edge. Let dry, then fit the two halves together for an egg unlike any you'll ever find in a nest!

✕

This is an example of a chain tale, where the various trades the boy makes are connected to one another like the links of a chain. Chain tales are very popular in parts of India, where the characters are often animals rather than people.

A Drum

here once was a poor widow who had only one child, a son. He was a kindhearted boy, always willing to help out in any way he could. Theirs was not an easy life, but the boy rarely complained. As long as he and his mother had each other, the boy didn't mind that his clothing was ragged or that he had only a few toys.

The boy had been secretly wishing for something, however. He had always wanted a drum. One day when his mother was going to the village to sell some of their grain, she asked, "Is there anything you would like from the market?"

The boy hesitated, then said, "All I would really like, Mother, is a drum. I know you won't be able to get me one, but that is what I would really like."

The boy was right. His mother knew she would never be able to buy a drum. The grain they grew and harvested to sell usually only gave her enough rupees, or Indian coins, to buy the few things she and her son could not grow or make themselves.

The poor woman thought of her son all the way home from the market, saddened that she was not able to get him the one thing he really wanted. She bent down to pick up a piece of wood she saw lying by the side of the road. "Perhaps my good son can find a use for this," she thought. "It's not much, but at least it's something."

1 The boy didn't know what to do with the wood when his mother gave it to him, but he thanked her and carried it with him when he went out to play.

Down the road, the boy could see an old woman kneeling beside a cookstove. The woman was trying to light the dried cow dung she used for fuel, but the fire wasn't catching and great billows of smoke hung all around her. Her eyes were watering, and the boy asked her why she was crying. "I can't get my fire to burn," she replied.

"Here," said the boy, handing her his piece of wood. "Perhaps this will help." In no time at all, the old woman was able to get the fire going. She thanked the boy, giving him a *chapati* (chah-PAH-tee), a round, flat bread, that she cooked in a pan on the stove.

The boy took the bread and walked on until he met another woman, this one the wife of the village potter. She held a small child in her arms, but the child was crying and could not be quieted. The boy spoke loudly so that he could be heard. "Why is your child crying?" he asked.

The potter's wife answered, "Because he is hungry. We have nothing for him to eat." The boy looked at the chapati he was holding in his hand, then offered it to the unhappy child. The child nibbled at the bread and stopped crying at once. By way of thanks, the grateful mother gave the boy a large pot.

The boy hadn't gone far when he came to the river, where he found a man and woman arguing. "What is the trouble?" asked the boy.

"I am a washerman," the man replied, "and my wife has just broken the only pot I had to boil clothes in. I'll never get the clothing clean now."

The boy realized that he had a solution to this man's problem, too, and gave the couple the pot he was carrying. "Thank you very much," the washerman said, and gave the boy a coat for his kindness.

The boy walked on further until he came to a man leading a horse along the road. The man wore sandals on his feet but was dressed in little more than his underclothes. His hair was wet, and he was shivering. The boy approached the man and asked, "What happened to your clothes, and why are you all wet?"

"I was on my way to visit relatives when a robber galloped up on this horse," the man replied. "He demanded I give him my clothes. Then he pushed me into the river."

The boy handed the man the coat he'd been given by the washerman. "Here," he said, "put this on." The man slipped on the garment. "Please take the horse," he told the boy. "The robber left it, and I have no need for it."

So the boy took the horse, and before long he came upon a wedding party—the bridegroom and his family, plus several musicians with their instruments. They were all seated beneath the shade of a small tree, looking not the least bit happy. "Why do you all look so glum?" the boy asked.

The father of the bridegroom spoke up. "We are waiting for the man who is bringing the horse my son will ride. But we don't know what has happened to this man, and if he doesn't arrive soon we shall be late for the wedding." (It was the custom for the groom to be on horseback during the wedding procession.)

The boy listened to this story, then offered the bridegroom his horse. "You have saved the day!" the groom exclaimed. Turning to speak with his father and one of the musicians, the groom handed the boy a drum. "Please accept one of our drums, with all of our thanks."

The boy's face lit up with joy. "Oh, thank you," he cried. "I have always wanted a drum. Thank you very much! And much happiness to you on your wedding day!"

The boy ran all the way home, as fast as his feet would take him. His astonished mother stared at the drum in disbelief as her son told her the entire story of how he had come to own it, starting with the piece of wood she had picked up along the side of the road.

They are there; we are here.

WHERE IN THE WORLD IS INDIA?

COUNTRY: **India**
CONTINENT: **Asia**
LANGUAGE: **Hindi, English**
CAPITAL: **New Delhi**
FLAG:

THE TAIL END OF A TALE

You might be wondering why the very last line of this story is "They are there; we are here." What can this possibly mean, and why is it at the end of the story?

Storytellers all over the world start—and end—tales in special ways to let their listeners know that what they are hearing are just that, stories. When you hear "once upon a time," you know you are about to be transported far from the real world, to a place where animals can talk and magical happenings are commonplace.

The same goes for the closing words of a story. The last sentence of "A Drum" is one of the ways storytellers in parts of India clue their listeners that the story is over. "They" are the characters of the story, living "there," in a world far from our own. We, the listeners, are reminded that "we are here."

Check to see some of the other ways stories begin and end in this book. Now, come up with your own ways to start and end a tale.

START

Once upon a time . . . No, wait! In a land far away there lived . . . hmm. Not bad. How about, In the time before? Or maybe, In the early days?...

And for an ending, They all lived happily ever—no everybody uses that one! Maybe, And life was forever thus in that faraway land. Yesss! I like it! The End!

FINISH

LINKED TOGETHER

You may be familiar with other chain tales, even some that are told in rhyming verse. Have you ever heard or read *I Know an Old Lady Who* *Swallowed a Fly* or *The House That Jack Built*? You could tell "A Drum" this way, too. Here's one way you might start the rhyme:

This is the boy who wan-ted a drum,

A drum he could tap with the end of his thumb.

This is the wood he found by the road,

The wood that was-n't much of a load

For the boy who wan-ted a drum,

A drum he could tap with the end of his thumb.

This is the wo-man start-ing the fire,

And so on . . .

Add to this rhyme, or make up your own. It's really easy to count the number of links when the story is told in this way, isn't it?

Many different types of breads are eaten in India, but because ovens are not very common, most breads are cooked on top of the stove.

Chapati is a popular stove-top bread in northern India, and one that you can easily make at home. Be sure to ask an adult to help you with any unfamiliar steps and when cooking at the stove.

Does chapati remind you of another popular bread that is cooked in this way? That's right, the Mexican tortilla is also a stove-top bread.

▼ ▼ ▼ ▼ ▼ ▼ ▼ ▼ ▼ ▼ ▼ ▼ ▼ ▼ ▼

Breadwinner

FOOD FOR THOUGHT · TALES ALIVE! RECIPE

1 Mix the two flours and salt together in a medium-sized bowl. Add the water, a little at a time, until the dough comes together into a ball. (If the dough is too crumbly, you may need to add a little more water, a teaspoonful at a time.) Knead the dough on a floured surface for about five minutes. Let the dough rest, under a kitchen towel, for 30 minutes.

2 Divide the rested dough into 12 pieces. Knead each piece briefly, then roll it out into a flat circle about 5 inches (15 cm) in diameter.

3 Meanwhile, have an adult heat a heavy griddle or frying pan on the stove over medium heat. When a drop of water sprinkled on the pan bounces and dances on the surface, the pan is hot enough. Carefully place a chapati on the griddle. Turn the chapati over when it begins to puff up, and cook the other side (for about half as long).

4 Keep the cooked chapatis warm in a basket lined with a kitchen towel. Serve with Indian food, such as a spicy curry. You can also spread butter and jam (or sprinkled sugar) on a chapati for a breakfast or snacktime treat.

Makes 12.

YOU'LL NEED
○ 1 ½ cups (200 g) whole wheat flour
○ ¾ cup (100 g) all-purpose flour
○ ¼ teaspoon (1-2 ml) salt
○ 1 cup (250 ml) water
○ Rolling pin

▲ ▲ ▲ ▲ ▲ ▲ ▲ ▲ ▲ ▲ ▲ ▲ ▲ ▲

TO THE BEAT OF A DIFFERENT DRUMMER

The drums Indian musicians play come in all sorts of shapes and sizes. Some are squat and bowl-shaped, others tall and skinny. There are even drums that are wide at both ends and narrow in the middle.

You can make one of these *waisted drums* (so called because the middle of the drum is like our waist) from a few items you may already have at home. Like the boy's mother in the tale, you'll be amazed how, by starting with two flower pots and a grocery bag, you end up with a drum!

1 Have an adult help you glue the two flower pots together at their bases. Let the glue dry overnight.
(PLEASE NOTE: *Only adults should handle household cement, because of potential dangers.*)

2 Cut open the grocery bag and cut two circles from the paper about 1 inch (2.5 cm) larger than the flower pot openings. Dampen one paper circle with water and center it over the open end of one of the pots. Hold the paper in place with the rubber band. Wrap moistened paper tape around the edge of the paper circle, pressing the tape down firmly to make it stick. Let the paper and paper tape dry completely before taping a paper circle to the other pot.

YOU'LL NEED

- ○ Terracotta flower pots, two the same size
- ○ Household cement
- ○ Heavy paper grocery bag
- ○ Rubber band
- ○ Gummed paper tape (the kind you moisten to make stick)
- ○ Scissors
- ○ Acrylic paints
- ○ Paintbrush

3 Decorate the drum with the paint, using some of the traditional Indian designs shown here or your own designs.

4 You'll notice how the paper shrinks as it dries, making the "drumheads" nice and tight. Use your hands to beat the drums, but take care not to tap too hard so you don't rip the paper.

✗

The following is an example of an explanation tale, a story that explains something about the natural world—in this case why hares always seem to be running. The Ewe (EH-vay) people of eastern Ghana have another reason for telling this tale. They use it to remind each other how all the members of a community must work together, even make sacrifices together, for the good of the community. It's a powerful message told in an entertaining way.

Why Hare Is Always on the Run

Listen to this story of the hare and the other animals of the bush.

It was very dry one year, with little rain. The trees lost their leaves and the grass turned brown. The crops in the fields withered and died. Over time, even the watering holes dried up. It was so bad that the animals called a meeting to see what could be done.

"There is nothing left to eat," agreed the animals, "and soon there will be no water either. What can we do to keep ourselves from dying of hunger and thirst?"

The animals talked among themselves for a long time. Then they reached a decision. Turtle stood before the assembly and announced, "So it shall be. We will all cut off the tips of our ears. Then we will squeeze all the fat from them. We will sell the fat, and, with the money we make, we will buy a hoe to dig a well. That way we will have water to quench our thirst and grow our crops."

So the animals all cut off the tips of their ears, all except Hare, who refused when it was his turn. The other animals didn't say anything. They did as they had planned, and, with the money they made from selling the fat squeezed from their ears, they bought a hoe.

As it turned out, that was a good plan. Before long, the animals had dug deep enough in the dried-up bed of the watering hole to strike water.

"Ha!" they said. "So now we can quench our thirst."

One by one the animals waited their turn to drink at the well, all except Hare, who was not there. He was on his way to the well, dragging a big calabash, or gourd, along the ground behind him. The calabash made an eerie sound. The calabash went *chan-gan-gan-gan, chan-gan-gan-gan. Chan-gan-gan-gan, chan-gan-gan-gan* it went.

The animals at the well looked up in fright when they heard the noise. "What is it?" they asked one another. No one knew. The sound grew louder and louder, until the animals could stand it no longer and ran away.

When Hare reached the well, he had it all to himself. He drank to his heart's content, then jumped into the water to cool his tired, dusty body.

The next day, the other animals cautiously returned to the well. There was no sign of the mysterious sound-maker, but the well water was muddy and unfit to drink.

"Who has spoiled our well water?" a gazelle cried.

"There's one way to find out," said a hyena. And working together, the animals made a life-size image of a hare from earth, covering it with sticky sap. They placed the image near the well, then ran and hid in the bush nearby.

When the sun was in the middle of the sky, Hare came along, dragging his calabash behind him. *Chan-gan-gan-gan, chan-gan-gan-gan* went the calabash. It went *Chan-gan-gan-gan, chan-gan-gan-gan.*

The animals saw who it was and nodded to one another but they didn't make a sound. Hare did not see them hidden in the bush.

When Hare saw the image of the hare, he motioned it away. "Be gone, if you know what's good for you," he said. But the dummy hare did not stir. Hare walked right up to it and declared, "Move on or I'll give you a slap."

When the dummy hare still did not move, Hare hit it squarely on its shoulder. His hand stuck fast in the sap. He struck the dummy with his other hand, but that one, too, got stuck.

"Take this then!" warned Hare, kicking out with both of his feet. But they stuck tight to the dummy, and Hare was unable to move a muscle to free himself.

The other animals came out of hiding. "So it was you," said Giraffe. "You, who refused to cut off the tips of your ears, even though you agreed to. You, who were nowhere to be found when it was time to dig the well. Yet you dirtied the well so the rest of us could not drink from it."

"You deserve to be punished," shouted the animals in anger. "We should toss you into jail and throw away the key. But we won't. Get out of here while you can, you wretched beast. Run, run, if you know what's good for you!"

The animals let Hare go, and he ran, he ran, he ran for all he was worth. And that is why the hare is always on the run.

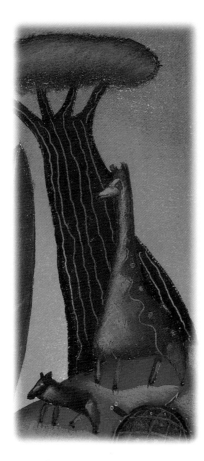

WHERE IN THE WORLD IS GHANA?

COUNTRY: **Ghana**
CONTINENT: **Africa**
LANGUAGE: **English, 8 major tribal languages**
CAPITAL: **Accra**
FLAG:

VARIATIONS ON A THEME

This same tale might have been told just slightly differently to explain why the hare has such long ears. After all, Hare was the only animal that refused to cut off his ear tips.

On the other hand, this story would have been told very differently had it come from another country. Even though many cultures share similar stories, a tale's characters and actions reflect that particular region's geography, climate, and customs.

You can play around with this yourself. Retell this tale so that it "sounds" like it comes from another country—a country that interests you or that you know something about. What do you have to change so that the story is a better reflection of life in that country?

IN A NUTSHELL

The meaning or message of many tales can be reduced to a single sentence or saying. Sayings such as these are called *proverbs*.

Take a proverb you may know—"An ounce of prevention is worth a pound of cure." What exactly does this mean? That it's better to take a little time to prevent problems rather than spend lots and lots of time later fixing curing them.

While many cultures share the meanings of proverbs, each culture tells proverbs in its own special way. Just as many African tales are about animals, so are many African proverbs. Here are a few sayings (and their meanings) of the Grebo people of Liberia in Africa:

Mosquito says, "If you want a person to understand you, buzz in his ears."
(Speaking directly to someone is more effective than sending them a written message.)

Alligator says, "We know the war canoe from the peace canoe."
(It is easy to tell harm from good.)

Hog says, "There are many muddy roads."
(If you are not successful going one way, try another way.)

How might you turn the message in "Why Hare Is Always on the Run" into a proverb? You can do the same with the other folktales in this book.

EXTRA! EXTRA!

Choose one of your favorite proverbs and write a complete story around it, a story that would explain how the proverb came to be. Do you think all proverbs started out as longer stories, or that all longer stories started out as proverbs?

NOT A DROP TO DRINK

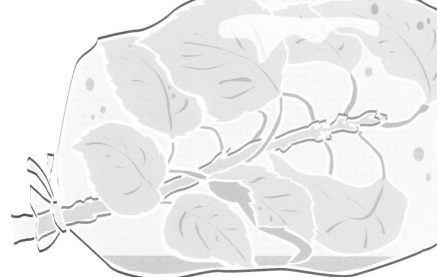

You can experiment collecting water from plants where you live. Tie a plastic bag around the end of a leafy branch of a bush or tree. The next day, check the bag. Are there droplets of moisture clinging to it? (It is best not to drink this water, as some plant leaves contain substances that are poisonous to humans.)

Most of us take water for granted. When we're thirsty, we just walk to the sink and fill a glass with cold water from the tap. When we need to wash our hands, our clothes, even the dishes, we turn on the water without even thinking about it. In parts of Africa, things are different. Water is scarce, and people have had to learn ingenious ways to collect it.

In remote regions where there are no wells, large, curved leaves are laid on the ground at sundown. The moisture in the air condenses overnight and is caught in the natural cup shape of the leaves.

In other places, the roots of certain plants are dug up. These are plants that have adapted to the dry climate by storing large amounts of water in their roots. The tips of the roots are cut off, and the moisture is squeezed from them.

All living plants contain water that is constantly evaporating into the air. (A large oak tree "gives off" as many as 300 gallons (1,135 l) of water vapor each day!) Try this plastic bag experiment with different tree leaves, at different times of year, and even with houseplants in your home. Do some plants produce more moisture than others? Why do you suppose this is?

MASK-MAKER, MASK-MAKER

Animals figure in a lot of African art, from clothing to ceremonial art. Perhaps you have seen some examples of African masks, many of which are made in the shapes of animals.

You can make your own animal masks, designed to be held in one hand with a stick.

- **Corrugated cardboard, the kind from cardboard boxes**
- **Ruler**
- **Scissors**
- **Poster paint**
- **Paintbrush**
- **¼-inch (.5 cm) dowel**
- **Masking tape**

ALL THE WORLD'S A STAGE

1 Cut a flat-topped oval out of the cardboard, larger than your face. Carefully bend the cardboard lengthwise. Mark the approximate location of your eyes and mouth, then take the cardboard away from your face and cut holes for these. The holes can be large and variously shaped, as shown in the examples here.

2 Cut out features, such as ears, nose, and whiskers, from extra pieces of cardboard. Glue the features in place. Paint the mask with the poster paints. Keep the design simple, so that it's easy to tell what your animal is, even from a distance.

3 Tape one end of the dowel in the groove at the back of the mask. Paint the dowel to match the mask, if you like.

If you make a set of masks for all the animal characters in the tale, you and a group of your friends can retell the story as a play. (The mouth holes in the masks will make it so you can be heard clearly when you hold a mask in front of your face.)

You'll probably want to gather up a few props, such as the hoe and the dummy hare (a stuffed toy bunny would work just fine). A small cardboard box pulled along the ground by a string could be Hare's noisy gourd. To make the bush the animals hide behind, stretch a blanket between two chairs. Then invite your audience to make themselves comfortable and watch you bring the tale to life.

While some people do not like the thought of hunting, many peoples around the world, including the Inuit, or Eskimos, once relied on animals for most of their food and clothing needs. Hunting was a matter of survival and, as this tale from the northern reaches of Canada describes, often dangerous.

Tuk the Hunter

his is the story of a boy named Tuk (took) who wanted to grow up to be a great hunter like his father.

Tuk was still too young to go on hunting trips, but he listened carefully to everything his father told him and was given many of the hunting chores. He helped ready the dogsled for each trip and had learned how to sharpen the hunting spears and knives. He practiced thrusting a spear and even knew how to cut up a carcass, throwing scraps to the dogs.

Tuk dreamt of the day when he would make his first kill. In his mind, he stalked not only the seals and walruses his father spoke of, but also that fearsome hunter, the polar bear. Tuk had given the big bear a nickname—White Monster.

Each evening when the work was done, Tuk took out his own little knife to carve soapstone toys. He made simple dolls his sister dressed in tiny sealskin clothes and animals of every kind. He carved sleek seals and killer whales, and even a tiny likeness of the White Monster. These are the animals I will hunt someday, Tuk thought as he carved.

At last the day came when his father announced that Tuk was ready to go on his first hunting trip. Together they packed the sled with food, spears, knives, and everything else they would need for the journey. Tuk was so excited he could hardly eat his morning meal.

"Eat up," Tuk's father advised. "We have a long day ahead of us, and you'll be glad you ate a good breakfast."

Tuk and his father tied the last things to the sled, then set off, waving good-bye to Tuk's mother and sister. They had not gone far when Tuk's father pointed to something in the distance. Straight ahead lay a fat seal with its back to them, sunning itself near an ice hole.

Tuk's father slowed the dogs and motioned to Tuk to stay behind in the sled. Then he jumped off the sled and onto his hands and knees. Tuk watched as his father crept silently toward the seal, his spear held ready in one hand.

Tuk's father was not the only one stalking the seal. From behind a snowbank appeared an enormous dirty-white polar bear. When it saw Tuk's father, it changed direction and began moving toward him, instead. Before Tuk could cry out a warning, the polar bear sprang at his father, knocking the spear out of his hand and pinning him to the ground.

Tuk grabbed an ax from the sled and ran toward the bear. "No, Tuk, keep away!" shouted his father. "Don't come near!"

But Tuk paid no attention and began swinging wildly at the polar bear with the ax. Holding Tuk's father with one paw, the bear tried to defend itself with the other. But it was unable to do both and, instead, rose on its hind legs with an angry growl and started after Tuk.

The boy turned and ran, dodging in and out of the snowbanks. He was just a few lengths ahead of the bear when he saw his father coming toward him on the dogsled.

"Quick, jump on!" Tuk's father commanded, and somehow Tuk was able to grab hold of the sled. They raced all the way back to the igloo, not daring to turn to see if the bear was following. When they reached the igloo, the dogs came to a quick stop. All the spears and knives rolled off the sled.

"Never mind," said Tuk's father, "we don't have time to pick them up. Quick, unharness the dogs and get them into the igloo."

Tuk did as he was told, then clambered in after them. Tuk's father was the last one in, quickly blocking up the igloo entrance with snow.

Tuk and his father told his mother and sister everything that had happened. They looked out one of the igloo's clear ice windows and saw that the polar bear had indeed followed Tuk and his father home. The huge beast was pacing back and forth, occasionally swiping at the igloo with his claws.

Tuk's father could do nothing, as all the spears and knives lay scattered outside on the ice. The family had no choice but to wait for the polar bear to leave.

The polar bear was still there the next morning and all the next day. Day after day the family waited until there was no food left for them to eat. Still the bear circled the igloo.

"We shall have to try and kill him," said Tuk's father one morning. "Either that or we'll end up starving." But Tuk persuaded his father to wait one more day, so that the bear might leave on its own.

That night, the moonlight streaming in through the ice window woke Tuk. He looked out and saw the polar bear some distance away, lying fast asleep.

With an idea forming in his mind, Tuk quietly got dressed. He picked up his little carving knife and crept out of the igloo.

Tuk stood up slowly and looked all around him. Then moving silently so as not to wake the bear, Tuk began to pack snow into a huge mound right near the tunnel entrance. When the snowbank was just the right size, Tuk took out his knife and began carving the mound.

He finished just as the sky was beginning to brighten. He stood back to survey his work, pleased with what he saw. There stood a polar bear made entirely from snow, so lifelike and fierce-looking that Tuk almost gasped.

Tuk knew it was just a matter of time before the polar bear was up, so he crawled feet-first back into the igloo tunnel to wait. Sure enough, minutes later, the bear awoke and stretched and moved sleepily over toward the igloo. But when it spied the snow bear, it reared up on its hind legs in surprise. This was the moment Tuk had been waiting for.

As swift as a snow owl dropping from the sky to capture its prey, Tuk leapt to his feet and threw himself at the bear, plunging his carving knife deep into the animal's chest. The creature howled in pain, swiping at Tuk with one paw, but not before Tuk was able to strike again. The bear let out one last roar, then collapsed in a heap.

The commotion had woken Tuk's father, who scrambled out of the igloo tunnel just in time to watch the polar bear fall to the ground. He smiled at Tuk, who was already carving up the dead animal for their first meal in days.

"From now on, you shall be known as Tuk the Hunter," his father said and proudly hugged his son.

WHERE IN THE WORLD IS CANADA?

COUNTRY: **Canada**
CONTINENT: **North America**
LANGUAGE: **English, French,
Eskimo languages**
CAPITAL: **Ottawa**
FLAG:

BELIEVE IT OR NOT

"Tuk the Hunter" is an exciting tale, the kind that leaves you on the edge of your seat, hoping everything turns out all right for the main characters. But it is a believable tale, too. Something like this could have happened, don't you think?

Maybe there really was an Inuit boy who killed a polar bear on his first hunting trip. It was something he would never forget for the rest of his life.

Maybe when this boy was a grown man he told the story to *his* son. And that boy grew up and told the story to his son, and so on and so on.

Do you have any family stories about amazing things that happened to your parents or grandparents, or even their grandparents? Ask the members of your family. You may be treated to some true stories that are as incredible—and memorable— as this one about brave Tuk.

Home, Sweet Home

The Inuit people living in north–central Canada are thought to have invented the snow house, what most people today call an *igloo*. Igloos were used as winter dwellings, while families lived in animal skin tents during the summer.

Just the right kind of snow— evenly packed and dense—is needed to make an igloo. The Inuit used a thin rod made from bone for testing the snow. When they found a good spot, a snow knife (originally made from a sharpened antler or bone) was used to cut out the blocks.

A family home meant to be used all winter long might take a few days to make. But an experienced igloo builder could construct a small, temporary igloo in less than an hour!

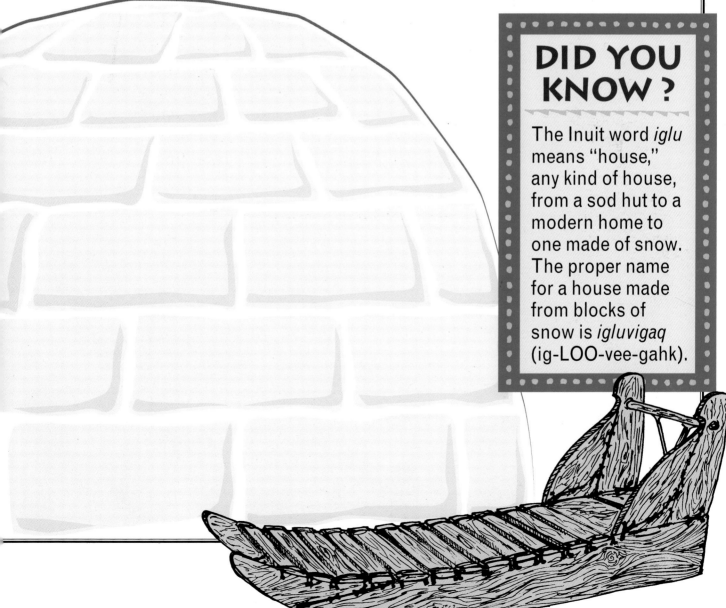

DID YOU KNOW ?

The Inuit word *iglu* means "house," any kind of house, from a sod hut to a modern home to one made of snow. The proper name for a house made from blocks of snow is *igluvigaq* (ig-LOO-vee-gahk).

SKILL BUILDER

Daily chores kept Inuit families busy inside their homes during the long winter nights. But when the work was done, there was always time for storytelling, making string figures, and playing games.

One of the most popular amusements was a toss-and-catch game the Canadian Inuit call *ajaqaq* (AH-jah-kahk). Played by both men and women (and boys and girls), the game was a great way to practice hand-eye coordination, a very important skill in hunting.

The tossing set was made from pieces of bone or walrus tusk tied together with sinew. You can make your own toss-and-catch toy from materials more commonly found where you live.

YOU'LL NEED

- 4 to 6 rubber canning rings
- Thick, cotton string
- Sturdy stick, about 12 inches (30 cm) long

1 Cut a piece of string about 18 inches (45 cm) long. Tie one end of the string securely to one ring. Thread the free end of the string through the remaining rings and then tie to the end of the stick.

2 To play the game, toss the rings in the air and try to "spear" them with the stick. You'll find it's not as easy as it looks!

GOOGLY GOGGLES

Anyone who has ever spent time playing in the snow on a sunny day knows how bright the sun's reflection on the snow can be—bright enough to hurt your eyes. In fact, *snow blindness* is a real concern, and it's a good idea to wear sunglasses to cut down the glare.

The Inuit also guarded against snow blindness, with ingenious goggles carved from bone or a walrus tusk. Shaped like a Halloween eye mask, with narrow slits instead of holes, these goggles helped reduce the amount of light hitting the eyes.

You can make your own pair of snow goggles.

1 Cut a narrow strip of poster board into a mask shape (or trace around an eye mask), then cut slits for your eyes. Color the front of the mask with the black marker, making sure to blacken around the inner rims of the slits, too. (It's important to use a permanent marker, because water-soluble ink will "run" if it gets wet.) Staple the elastic to either side of the goggles, adjusting it for a comfortable fit.

2 Compare what it is like on a sunny day with and without the goggles on. Which is easiest on your eyes?
(Note: With or without goggles, never look directly at the sun—its rays can permanently damage your eyes.)

YOU'LL NEED

○ **Poster board**
○ **Scissors**
○ **Black permanent marker**
○ **Elastic**
○ **Stapler**

CHIP OFF THE OLD BLOCK

Tuk carved his sister's dolls and his animals out of *soapstone*, a rock that's also known as steatite. How do you think it got the nickname soapstone? You guessed it—because it's so soft!

You can try your hand at carving using a bar of real soap. Experiment with different types of soap, from your basic white bar to super-soft glycerin soap. As your carving skills improve and you no longer want your first attempts, "retire" them…to the soap dish, of course!

- **Rectangular bath-size bar of soap**
- **Pencil or toothpick**
- **Blunt knife, such as a butter knife**

WASTE NOT, WANT NOT

1 Plan your design on paper first. Simple shapes are the easiest to carve. Remember a sculpture has six sides: the top, the bottom, the front, the back, and the two sides. Transfer your design to the soap bar, drawing the outline of your animal on all sides of the bar with a pencil or toothpick.

2 Cut away everything outside the lines you've drawn on the soap. While it is a good idea to cut away from yourself, sometimes you'll have better control cutting toward yourself, with the dull knife held firmly, as shown.

3 Add details if you like, such as lines to show legs or tiny holes for eyes. You can also scratch short lines all over the animal's body to show its fur.

SNOW BEASTS

Naturally, if you live where it snows, you can make a larger version of your soap carving out of the white stuff. Turn your front lawn into a habitat for all sorts of Arctic animals. Sea lions and foxes, and bears, oh my!

The Inuit were careful never to let anything go to waste. They used every part of the animals they killed for food and other purposes. The warm hides were tanned and sewn into blankets and clothing; the sinew was twisted and made into rope and string. Even the tusks and bones were used for everything from sewing needles to harpoon heads.

So, don't waste the soap shavings from your "soapstone" carvings. Put all the bits and pieces in a small bowl with a little water. Form the wet mass into a round soap ball, then set it aside for a few days to dry. Use it as you would any bar of soap.

✕

This is a classic noodlehead or numbskull tale, named for the foolish characters who believe just about everything Campriano the farmer tells them. As for Campriano, he's not quite the fool people take him for!

The Story of Campriano

here was once a farmer named Campriano. Each day he could be seen tending the grapes in his vineyard or turning over the soil in the fields with the help of a tired old mule. Campriano usually kept to himself and didn't have much to say to the other farmers. Perhaps that was why they said, "Campriano is such a simpleton. It's a wonder he is able to put enough food on his table."

Most days when the work was done, the farmers left the fields together. They talked loudly, boasting about the size of their harvests and the abilities of their animals. Campriano rarely joined in. "Campriano has nothing to boast about," the other farmers would say among themselves.

One morning before setting out to work, Campriano fed his mule a handful of gold coins he had saved. The mule worked all morning long, and all afternoon, too, and then it was time to go home.

Campriano left the fields just as two neighboring farmers who often teased him were leaving. Campriano's mule stopped along the lane, leaving a pile of droppings on the road. The two farmers stopped and stared at the pile in disbelief.

"Campriano!" one of the farmers exclaimed. "Your mule's droppings are full of money!"

"Oh, I know," replied Campriano, with a perfectly straight face. "I don't know what I'd do without my mule. He's a real treasure."

"You must sell your mule to us," insisted the two farmers.

"Oh, I could never do that," answered Campriano.

"Are you asking too much for him?" one of the farmers wanted to know. "Is that why you won't sell him to us?"

"Oh, it's not that," said Campriano.

"Then we'll give you five hundred crowns for him," the two farmers offered.

Campriano thought about this for a minute, then said, "Fine." Between them, the two farmers came up with five hundred crowns and led the mule away.

When they got home the two farmers were excited. They called their wives to the barn and told them to spread bedsheets on the floor to catch all the gold pieces that the mule would drop during the night.

The next morning the farmers raced to the barn, only to discover the sheets covered with manure. "We've been tricked!" the two men

shouted. "Campriano will pay for this!" Grabbing two pitchforks, the farmers set off in the direction of Campriano's house.

Campriano's wife answered the door. "My husband isn't here," she told the enraged farmers. "He's working in the vineyards."

The two farmers marched out to the vineyards, madder than ever. "You cheat, you liar, you scoundrel!" they shouted at Campriano. "We should have you arrested for what you've done to us!"

"Come, come, neighbors," Campriano calmly replied. "What seems to be the trouble?"

"Your mule is a worthless animal. He makes piles of droppings like any other mule," one farmer said. Campriano looked puzzled, then asked, "What did you feed the beast?"

"Only the best fresh grass and cold water from the spring," the farmers replied.

"Why, there you have it," said Campriano. "My mule doesn't eat what other mules eat. He's used to eating stalks and rough grass that turn into hard coins. I certainly hope this doesn't spell the end of this good mule," he added, looking concerned. "Let me come and have a look at him. If he's all right, I'll take him back and return your money. But if any harm has come to him, I'm afraid that he is your problem and our deal stands."

"Agreed," said the two farmers.

"I'll meet you at your barn in just a few minutes," Campriano said. "I just want to stop by my house to let my wife know where I'll be."

When Campriano reached his house, he told his wife, "You must do something for me. Boil up a pot of soup on the stove. When I come home for lunch, take the pot from the cupboard, as though it has been cooking there."

Campriano met the two farmers at their barn. "Oh, this doesn't look good," he said when he had seen his mule. "I'm surprised the poor beast is still alive. If only I had known what you would feed him."

"What do we do now?" the farmers wailed.

"I'm afraid there is nothing to be done. This is your problem, as you agreed. But so that there are no hard feelings, come join me for lunch at my house. My wife is a wonderful cook."

The two farmers accompanied Campriano to his house, but his wife was not there. Campriano stepped outdoors and called his wife's name. She came from the hen house, pretending to have just finished her chores there. "I have invited our neighbors to join us for lunch," Campriano told her.

"Oh, I wish I had known they were coming," said Campriano's wife. "I would have prepared something special. No matter," she added. "We'll just have some soup." And with that, Campriano's wife set the table and opened the cupboard, taking out the steaming hot soup pot.

"What!" the two farmers exclaimed in surprise. "A pot of soup that cooks by itself in the cupboard? How does it do that without any fire underneath it?"

"Oh, I don't know what we would do without this soup pot," said Campriano, without batting an eye. "It makes workdays so much easier for my wife and me. We know there will always be a nice pot of soup ready and waiting when we come in to eat."

"You must sell us the pot," declared the two farmers. "Things didn't work out with the mule, and this will help make up for it. We'll give you another five hundred crowns for the soup pot."

"Well, I suppose that's only fair," said Campriano, and the two farmers left with the pot.

Of course, the two farmers were not a bit happy when they discovered they had been fooled again. They stormed back to Campriano's house, fists upraised.

"We're taking no chances with you," they told Campriano, throwing him into a big grain sack that they tied closed with a big knot. They ran a stout pole through the knot, and each took an end of the pole and hoisted it on their shoulders.

Where were the farmers headed? To the pond near the village tavern. Only they were thirsty after carrying their heavy load and decided to stop and have a cold drink in the tavern. Campriano felt himself being lowered to the ground, and when he could tell that the two farmers had entered the tavern, he started moaning, "I won't have her! I tell you, I won't have her!"

A young farmer leading a cow was walking past when he heard Campriano's cries. The farmer looked puzzled, but when Campriano repeated, "I won't have her," the young farmer bent down near the sack and asked, "Who won't you have?"

"The king's daughter," replied Campriano from inside the sack. "The king wants me to marry his daughter, but I really can't do it. Oh, she's beautiful, and she dresses in jewels from head to toe, but I can't marry her. I am just a simple farmer, and a simple farmer I want to stay."

"You say the princess is beautiful and you say she is rich?" asked the young farmer. "I'd do anything to be in your shoes!"

"Well, that's easy enough," Campriano offered. "Take my place in this sack. I'm sure the king would much prefer you as a son-in-law, seeing as you are at least willing."

"I'm willing, all right!" exclaimed the young farmer, undoing the sack's knot. "You may as well take my cow," he added, "as I'll have no need for her now." And with that Campriano traded places with the young farmer and led the cow away.

When the two farmers came out of the tavern they picked up their bundle and carried it to the pond's edge. "Good riddance!" they shouted as they tossed the sack into the water. (A very wet and angry young man was seen leaving the pond not much later.)

The two farmers were certainly surprised when they got home to see Campriano leading his new cow. "Campriano, is that you?" questioned one of the farmers. "Where did you get that nice-looking cow?"

asked the other.

"You'll never guess," replied Campriano. "Did you know that the tavern pond leads to the Land of Plenty? I had always heard this was so, but I never believed it until I saw it with my very own eyes. Why, I came away with just this one cow, but there are hundreds more like her still down there."

"Free?" asked the farmers.

"Absolutely free," replied Campriano.

The two foolish farmers hardly heard Campriano's last words. They turned and ran down the road to the tavern pond as fast as their legs would take them. They were last seen diving into the pond. What happened to them? No one knows for sure, but they were never seen in those parts again.

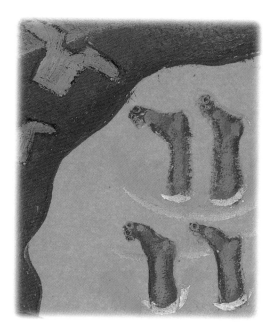

COUNTRY: **Italy**
CONTINENT: **Europe**
LANGUAGE: **Italian**
CAPITAL: **Rome**
FLAG:

TRICKS OF THE TRADE

You weren't fooled by Campriano's claims that his mule's droppings were made of gold or that his soup pot cooked all by itself. You may not be fooled by the following science tricks, either, but you'll have to admit they're pretty amazing.

These simple experiments demonstrate basic physical properties of water and air, plus one of the surprising shortcomings of the human brain. Once you've seen how these experiments work, see if you can trick your family members and friends!

CAN YOU TIE WATER IN KNOTS?

With the help of an adult, hammer five holes near the bottom of an empty coffee can. The holes should be about ¼ inch (.5 cm) apart. Fill the can with water at the sink. Notice how a stream of water comes out each of the five holes.

Pinch the five streams of water together with your fingers, near the holes. The streams should come together, looking as if they are tied in knots.

How does this work?

The strong force called *surface tension* binds water, and in this experiment causes the five streams to flow as one. Try brushing your hand across the water near the container. What happens?

BET YOU CAN'T LIFT THIS PAPER!

Lay a large sheet of paper, like a double sheet from a newspaper, on one corner of a table. Slip a ruler (either a long or short one) under the paper so that about a third of the ruler hangs over the table edge. Hit the end of the ruler with your hand. Can you lift the paper?

How does this work?

Why couldn't you budge the paper? *Air pressure*, plain and simple. Because the paper has a large surface area, there is a lot of air pressing down on it—enough, in fact, to make it almost impossible to lift the paper in this way, even though you hit the ruler with some force.

CAN YOU PUT A TISSUE IN WATER AND HAVE IT STAY DRY?

Fill a sink with water. Crumple up a facial tissue and put it into the bottom of a small drinking glass. Turn the glass upside down and push it completely underwater. Lift the glass up and check the tissue. It should be dry.

How does this work?

The tissue stays dry because water can't get into the glass. Why? Because the glass is full of *air*. The air can't get out of the glass because air is lighter than water. As you probably noticed, holding the glass vertically when it is put into the water is important so that the air cannot escape.

CAN YOU BORE A HOLE IN YOUR HAND?

Hold a cardboard paper towel tube (or a rolled-up sheet of paper) against your right eye. Place your open left hand right up against the side of the tube, palm facing you. Can you see a big hole going right through your hand?

How does this work?

Yikes! Where did that hole come from? Your right eye sees what's through the tube, while your left eye sees your open palm. Your brain receives both signals and can't sort them properly. The best it can do is combine the signals into this rather unusual sight. And to think that you saw it with your own two eyes!

GAME OF GOOSE

Have you ever heard anyone say, "Don't be such a goose!"? Goose is sometimes used to mean simpleton or fool. Goose is also the name of a popular board game from Italy, enjoyed by children throughout the world.

In this classic game of chance, each roll of the dice sends players along a spiral of marked squares. Getting to the finish is not as easy as it looks!

1 Using a pencil (and the ruler, if you like), draw the spiraling design shown on a piece of poster board. Go over all the lines with the black marker, then color the background around the squares black.

2 Use the marker to draw simple designs on each square to symbolize the different actions the players must take. You might draw a pair of dice to show that a player gets an extra turn. Draw an arrow to show that a player moves forward or backward (depending on the direction of the arrow) the same number of squares as the dice throw. Draw an upraised hand or a stop sign to mark those squares where a player loses a turn.

3 Decorate all the remaining squares with a goose (of course!), then number all the squares. Color the squares with crayons, markers, or paint.

4 To play the game, have each player roll the two dice and move according to the roll and the instructions on the board. The first player to land directly on the finish square is the winner, but he must land on an exact throw. If the player rolls a higher number than needed, he has to move back that number of squares and try again.

YOU'LL NEED

- Poster board
- Pencil
- Ruler
- Black marker with a fine tip
- Crayons, markers, or paint
- Four plastic milk bottle caps in different colors, or other play pieces
- Pair of dice

What type of soup do you suppose Campriano and his wife and neighbors ate for lunch that day? Perhaps they enjoyed one of the best-known Italian soups, minestrone (min-ess-TROH-nay), which means "big soup."

Here's a simplified version of minestrone you and your family may enjoy. While you won't be able to cook this delicious soup in your cupboard, you will find most of the ingredients for it in there! Have an adult help you with any steps you are not familiar with, and when cooking on the stove.

Soup of the Day

1 Pour the can of stewed tomatoes into a bowl. Using a potato masher or a knife (have an adult help you with the knife), mash or cut the tomatoes into small pieces. Place the stewed tomatoes, water, and bouillon cubes in a large saucepan. Heat on the stove until the mixture comes to a boil and the bouillon cubes have completely dissolved.

2 Carefully add the pasta to the broth. Bring the broth back to a gentle boil, stirring occasionally to make sure the pasta doesn't stick to the bottom of the pan. Cook for about 10 minutes, or until the pasta is done.

YOU'LL NEED

- 1 15-ounce (425 g) can Italian-style stewed tomatoes
- 6 cups (1.5 liters) water
- 6 chicken bouillon cubes
- ½ cup (35 g) small pasta shapes, such as ditali or elbow macaroni
- 1 15-ounce (425 g) can kidney beans
- 1 15-ounce (425 g) can mixed vegetables
- Grated Parmesan cheese

3 Meanwhile, open the cans of vegetables and wash and drain them. When the pasta is done, add the vegetables to the pot, stirring until they are heated through. Ladle the soup into deep bowls and sprinkle with the grated Parmesan cheese.

Makes 6 generous servings.

The hare in this tale is not what she seems, but you may have guessed that already from the title. While this Scottish tale can be enjoyed any time of year, reading it by candlelight on the last day of October is especially appropriate.

The Blue-Eyed Hare

t the edge of the moor there once lived a lad who was a beekeeper. Everyday he would stroll among his hives, talking to his bees and fussing over them. People in those parts claimed the bees could understand what the lad said, and that he, in turn, understood them. Maybe there was some truth in that.

One day as the lad was returning to his cottage for his evening meal, he was surprised to find a wee hare sitting on the stoop. The creature wasn't a bit timid and stood still when the beekeeper bent down to stroke her fur. He opened the door to his home, and the hare hopped right into the cottage. And she kept hopping, until she'd hopped onto a chair and onto the table, and made herself comfortable right next to the beekeeper's plate!

The beekeeper noticed there was something unusual about this hare. Her eyes weren't brown, nor were they pink; instead they were as blue as a cloudless sky on a summer's day.

"You're a lovely thing," the lad said to the hare. "I don't know what brings you here, but you are welcome to stay." And so began a most unusual friendship between man and beast.

The next day the lad introduced the hare to his bees. For as any beekeeper will tell you, bees insist on knowing everything that's going on where they live. Either that, or they'll up and move elsewhere. The lad carried the hare from hive to hive, stopping at each. The bees buzzed around the creature's head, but she was no more frightened of them than she was of the beekeeper.

That afternoon an old woman stopped at the beekeeper's cottage. At first, the lad thought she had probably come to buy some honey, but the old woman had eyes only for the hare.

"That's a fine looking hare you have there," she said. "How much are you asking for her?"

"This hare is not for sale," the lad replied.

"I'll make it well worth your while," the woman went on, taking out a bag of coins and handing the beekeeper a fistful of florins.

"I'll tell you again," the lad said firmly, "I don't intend on selling this hare."

A few bees had been hovering near the beekeeper, and off they flew to the hives. A moment later a large swarm of bees returned and began buzzing angrily around the old woman. She started to back away, then turned and ran. "Keep a close eye on that hare, lad," she warned as she disappeared from view.

From then on, the beekeeper kept the hare with him at all times. She even went to town with him on market day. On one such day the beekeeper was startled to see the old woman walking about the village square. He asked one of the other merchants who she was.

"They say she's a witch," whispered the merchant, making the sign of the cross. Well, the lad had no way of knowing if this were true or not, but he decided to keep an even closer watch on the hare, just in case.

The summer days gradually grew shorter and autumn finally arrived. The colder weather slowed the bees' activity, and the beekeeper knew that soon they would not be leaving the warmth and protection of their hives. The shorter days were sending the birds south, too, and before long the wandering gypsies would follow.

One crisp day in early October, a brightly colored gypsy caravan pulled by a bony horse lumbered past the cottage. The beekeeper looked up and waved in greeting. Only when the wagon was out of sight did he notice that something had fallen from it onto the road. It was a sack of grain, no doubt feed for the horse. With the hare under one arm, and the sack of grain upon his shoulder, the beekeeper set off after the gypsies.

An hour later he caught up with the wagon, pulled over beside the lane beneath the shade of some trees. The beekeeper could tell from the delicious smells coming from the wagon that the gypsies were having their midday meal.

"Hallo," called the beekeeper. "Is there anyone home?"

A gypsy lad poked his head out of the window of the caravan. "What is it you want?" he asked suspiciously.

"Only to return this sack of grain that fell from your wagon," replied the beekeeper.

"Oh, thank you," the gypsy said, recognizing the beekeeper now. Only then did the gypsy lad notice the hare that the beekeeper had tucked in the crook of his arm. "What have you there?" he asked.

"A hare," laughed the beekeeper. "Surely you've seen a hare before."

"Never one with blue eyes," the gypsy replied. "Grandmother," he called, "come see what this lad has with him."

A wizened woman with a shawl draped over her head appeared at the window. Her eyes narrowed as she gazed first at the hare and then at the beekeeper.

"That is no hare," she said with certainty. "You've got yourself a lassie who's been bewitched."

And then the beekeeper understood. He told the gypsies how the hare had arrived on his doorstep, and about the old woman who appeared the next day wanting to buy her.

"You've not seen the last of that witch," the gypsy woman warned. "All Hallows' Eve is approaching. That's when witches have their greatest powers."

She paused for a moment, then continued. "One good turn deserves another, we always say. I'll tell you what you can do, but you'll need your bees' help." The old gypsy woman outlined a plan. The lad thanked her, then headed home.

On All Hallows' Eve, the last day of the month, the beekeeper did just as the old gypsy woman had instructed. He went from hive to hive asking the bees to help him that night. Then he picked up the hare and climbed into his wagon. Giving the reins a shake, they set off.

On and on they went, never pausing, as day melted into evening and evening into night. The full moon was so bright the beekeeper's pony had no trouble keeping to the lane. All the while the lad kept a firm hold on the hare.

Then suddenly the hare gave a jerk and began to wriggle and twitch. The lad knew it must be midnight and that the witch was using all her powers to reclaim the hare. The beekeeper tightened his grasp.

For a moment he feared he had lost the hare when a dark cloud swept in front of the moon. But when the clouds parted, the lad was still holding tight, but instead of a hare he held a lovely, blue-eyed lass in his arms. The lassie told the beekeeper how she had come to be under the wicked witch's spell.

That Sunday the two were wed at the village church. On market day the newlyweds rode into town with their honey. The merchant

who had pointed out the witch took the beekeeper aside.

"What do you make of this?" he asked the beekeeper. "That wicked woman you were asking about was found dead last week at the edge of the moor."

"How did she meet her end?" inquired the beekeeper.

"The doctors couldn't be sure, but it appeared as if she'd been stung to death by bees." The merchant paused. "Strange," he said, "seeing how there are no bees about this time of year."

The beekeeper smiled to himself. "Strange things are known to happen," was all he said in reply.

WHERE IN THE WORLD IS SCOTLAND?

COUNTRY: **Scotland**
CONTINENT: **Europe**
LANGUAGE: **English**
CAPITAL: **Edinburgh**
FLAG:

CHANGING FORM

In this story, a young woman, or lassie, is turned into a hare, and later back into her human form. This kind of change is found in lots of tales told around the world. Just think of some of the other stories where this happens, such as "Beauty and the Beast" or "The Frog Prince."

You aren't likely to ever experience the kind of *transformation,* or change, the lassie underwent, but you have seen some amazing changes in your life. Just think how you've grown in the last year or since you started school, or even since you were born!

For proof of those changes, take a look at some of your baby pictures and snapshots taken over the years. You've done a lot more than grow in size, of course. Ask an adult how old you were when you said your first word or took your first steps. They can remind you of other big milestones, such as when you learned to ride a two-wheeled bicycle, to read, or to get your own breakfast in the morning.

And there are more exciting changes to come, as you mature into a teenager, a young adult, and beyond. This transformation may not be as fantastic as the lassie's, but the growth and changes we all experience in our lifetime are every bit as remarkable.

A Night to Remember

No doubt you've guessed that All Hallows' Eve is another name for Halloween. (Hallowe'en—as it's sometimes spelled—is a contraction of Hallow Even, "even" being short for evening.) Did you know that this holiday got its start in the British Isles more than 2,000 years ago?

How people celebrate the holiday has changed over the years, but one thing hasn't changed much— Halloween is still a night for magic, superstition, and fun!

If you are like most kids, you enjoy dressing up and going to a party or from house to house, asking for treats. But the fun doesn't have to end there! Here are two Halloween activities that may become an annual tradition in your home.

Witches' Brew

Concoct a "witches' brew" to warm you up when you get home from trick-or-treating. Have an adult help you with any steps you are not familiar with and when heating the cider on the stove.

YOU'LL NEED

- ○ 2 quarts (2 liters) apple cider
- ○ Large cooking pot
- ○ Orange
- ○ Grater
- ○ 2 cinnamon sticks
- ○ Wooden stirring spoon

1 Pour the apple cider into the cooking pot. Grate the outer skin of the orange. Put the grated peel and the cinnamon sticks into the pot, stirring well.

2 Heat the cider on the stove until it is warm. Recite the following lines from *Macbeth,* a play by William Shakespeare (set in Scotland!), as you and your friends and family take turns stirring the pot:

Double, double, toil and trouble,
Fire burn and cauldron bubble.

Makes 12 6-ounce (175 ml) servings.

FOOD FOR THOUGHT · TALES ALIVE! RECIPE

Beeswax Candles

Make rolled beeswax candles, using flat sheets of beeswax that can be found in many craft stores. Remember: You should light and burn candles with adult supervision only.

YOU'LL NEED
○ Sheet of beeswax
○ Cotton wicking
○ Scissors

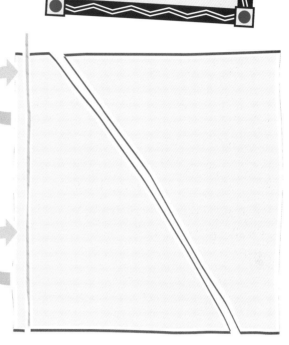

1 To roll a tapered candle, one that is fat at one end and skinnier at the other, cut a square sheet of beeswax in half, diagonally, as shown. Set aside one of the pieces.

2 Cut a piece of wicking about an inch longer than the vertical edge of the beeswax. Place the wick along this edge and carefully fold the beeswax over it, pressing the wax to hold the wick in place. Using the palms of both hands, roll the beeswax into a tight cylinder. Gently press down the edge of the wax so that it lies flat along the length of the candle.

3 Do the same with the other piece of beeswax. Place your dripless candles in candleholders (the fat end can be pinched to fit into most holder openings) before lighting and burning.

WICKED!

In this story the wicked old woman who casts a spell on the lassie is believed to be a witch. Witches and other beings with powerful magic are found in lots of tales from around the world.

Russian tales tell of Baba Yaga, a wicked old witch who lives in a home perched high on a huge pair of chicken legs. In Scandinavian folktales, the powerful, feared creature is usually a troll—sometimes described as a giant, other times as a dwarf. Japanese lore is full of mention of demonlike characters, including the mischievous *tengu* (TEHN-goo). These make-believe creatures like to play tricks on humans and are forever changing shape themselves.

If you were to invent a wicked being, what would it be like? Draw a picture of your creation and give it a suitable name. What makes your wicked being special, or especially fearsome?

HANDY PUPPET

The beekeeper found the blue-eyed hare good company, quiet as she was. After all, she couldn't speak—at least not until she was turned back into a beautiful, blue-eyed lassie.

This simple hand puppet in the shape of a hare will happily keep you company. You'll have to supply the voice for your hare, but you'll notice that its mouth certainly opens up nice and wide!

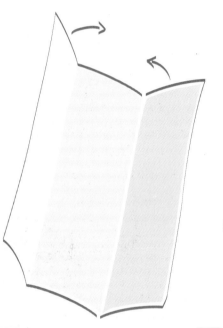

1 Fold the sheet of construction paper in thirds, lengthwise.

2 Fold this in half, then fold the top layer of each half back at its midpoint. Slip your thumb into one opening, and your fingers into the other to see how the puppet's mouth works.

3 Cut the hare's features from the paper scraps—long ears, eyes, and teeth—and glue them in position.

Note: Let your imagination go wild, and make other animal—and monster—puppets. Experiment with googly eyes on folded paper springs. Decorate with glitter and other add-ons.

YOU'LL NEED

○ **Construction paper, one sheet at least 9 inches by 12 inches (23 cm x 30.5 cm), plus scraps in various colors**
○ **Scissors**
○ **White glue**

SWEET STUFF

No one knows when our ancestors first tasted honey, but you can be sure they liked what they licked off their fingers when they reached into a tree hollow to see what those busy bees were up to. No doubt they quickly learned that the bees should be temporarily removed from the hive before collecting the honey!

Honey was gathered from the wild for centuries before someone had the idea to "keep" bees in artificial hives. Wall decorations in an Egyptian temple dating from around 2600 B.C. show beekeepers at work, and the Romans, centuries later, turned beekeeping into quite a science. They were mistaken about a few things, however. For one, they called the queen bee the king!

Did you know that honey comes in all sorts of flavors and colors, depending on the flowers from which the bees have gathered their nectar? If you have any honey in your house, check to see what kind it is. The label may say it's clover honey, one of the most popular kinds, or buckwheat honey, a very dark and strong-tasting honey. What other types of honey have you heard of or tried?

Honey in the Morning...

You can turn your favorite honey into a treat known as honey butter. This is delicious spread on toast, or dolloped on a stack of pancakes or waffles.

YOU'LL NEED

- ¼ cup (55 ml) honey
- 2 tablespoons (31 g) butter or margarine, at room temperature
- 2 tablespoons (30 ml) whipping cream

Mix the three ingredients together in a small bowl. Cover and refrigerate any leftovers, but bring it to room temperature before using.

Makes about ½ cup (125 ml).

The tribesmen of Arnhem Land, the Aboriginal reservation
located in Australia's Northern Territory, where this tale is told, have
many myths about the natural world. This particular myth explains
why the morning star shines so brightly.

Lighting the Way

n the dreamtime, the spirit girl, Barnumbir (BAR-num-beer), lived on the Island of the Dead. She was a happy girl, content to do her many daily chores, but she always made time to spend with her friends.

Barnumbir's friends shared many of her interests, save one. While those girls often went fishing with the men in their bark canoes, Barnumbir preferred to stay on land. She would swim in the shallow waters close to shore, but she never journeyed out on the water. She said it was because she had once dreamt that her spirit had been lost out on the ocean, and that is why she feared the deeper waters.

One day Barnumbir's two closest friends, two sisters, announced that they would soon be leaving on a sea voyage with their brother, who was planning on making his home far from the Island of the Dead. When Barnumbir heard this, she was greatly saddened. "You are my closest friends," she told the sisters. "Please don't go. I shall miss you terribly."

The two sisters hugged their friend. "We don't wish to leave, either," they said, "but our brother needs us. We must help him make the long journey by boat, and then we will stay to help him build his home. We must go with our brother."

Barnumbir thought for a moment and then announced, "I will go with you. I am afraid of the sea, but I cannot bear the idea of your leaving."

The two sisters smiled but shook their heads. "There is only room for three in our boat. You will have to stay behind."

Barnumbir was determined to go with her friends but did not know how she would manage to accompany them on their sea voyage. She asked others on the island if there was a larger canoe that could carry all of them, but was told that her friends' canoe was the longest there was. She offered to paddle another canoe alongside her friends' boat, but was told that the strength of one girl would not be enough.

Then someone suggested that Barnumbir visit Djanlin (JAHN-lin), the magician. Perhaps he would turn her into a star that could light the way for her friends' canoe. She considered this for a time. Finally, unable to think of any other way she could go with her friends, Barnumbir went to Djanlin.

"Is it true that you can make me into a star that can travel through the air just above my friends' canoe?" she asked the magician.

"Yes," Djanlin replied. "I can sing a magic song and make you a star."

He looked directly at Barnumbir, and then continued, "But you must know something. When you are no longer in sight of the Island of the Dead, I will have no way of calling you back. You will have to stay a star forever and forever travel over the water. You must think this over carefully before you decide."

Barnumbir was even more confused. She went to ask the advice of two wise old women on the island. The women sat on the ground rolling fibers of pandanus root between their hands and thighs. They coiled this thin rope round and round, forming it into a large basket that sat between them.

"Please, I need your help," Barnumbir said to the old women. "I wish to become a star to help guide my friends as they journey across the sea. Djanlin the magician has said that he can sing his magic and make me a star, but that when I am no longer in sight of our island, he will not be able to bring me back home. What shall I do?"

The two women sat in silence for a long time. They continued rolling the pandanus root fibers and building the sides of the basket. At last one of them spoke. "We must think this over. Come back tomorrow and we will have something to tell you."

Barnumbir returned to the old women's hut the next morning. She could hardly wait to hear what the wise ones would say, but she waited until one of them spoke first.

"We have considered your problem," one woman said. "We can help you. The way we see it, the sun will light the way for your friends by day. At night the stars high in the heavens will guide them. It is during the early morning hours that your friends will need a light the most."

The woman fell silent. The other woman spoke. "Let Djanlin the magician make his magic so that you can float as a star above your friends' canoe each morning."

"But what will become of me when I am far from the Island of the Dead?" asked Barnumbir, fearful that the old women, in fact, could not help her.

"We shall tie a long piece of rope to you," replied the first old woman. "When the sun has awakened from his sleep, we will pull you back to this basket. You will remain here on the island with your people each day and each night, but we will let out the rope just before the night stars have faded, so that you may light the way for all those who wander about in the early morning hours."

And so it is to this day. Just before dawn, you can spot the morning star in the sky. Her light is small but bright. Once the sun is up, Barnumbir's work is over and she is gone, back to the Island of the Dead where she still lives.

WHERE IN THE WORLD IS AUSTRALIA?

COUNTRY:	**Australia**
CONTINENT:	**Australia**
LANGUAGE:	**English, Aboriginal languages**
CAPITAL:	**Canberra**
FLAG:	

IN THE BEGINNING

The Aborigines of Arnhem Land tell many tales about supernatural spirits that lived long ago during a time they call *alcheringa* (al-CHE-ring-ah), "the dreamtime." The stories are filled with characters like Barnumbir and Djanlin. According to traditional Aboriginal beliefs, supernatural spirits such as these created the world and everything on it.

Each clan, or extended family, is believed to be descended from one of these dreamtime spirits. A clan's ancestor might be the spirit that became a certain fish in the ocean, or the eucalyptus tree, or the morning star itself.

The members of a clan are said to possess some of the life force of their ancestral spirit, and they have a special feeling for that part of nature created by the spirit. A person who is descended from a certain fish will not eat that fish, for instance. A clan whose ancestor was a tree will thank their ancestral spirit whenever using the tree in some way.

If you could choose some part of the natural world to be your "ancestor," what would you choose? What kind of special meaning does that part of nature have for you?

NIGHT AND DAY

Barnumbir's guiding light would have been needed at different times of the day, depending on the season that her friends made their sea voyage. In summer, as you know, daylight comes very early in the morning, perhaps before you even wake up. In the middle of winter, it's just the opposite. It may still be pitch black when you get out of bed to get ready for school.

Have you ever kept track of the time the sun rises—and sets—each day? This is something you can easily do in the form of a chart. The illustration shows one way you can chart the times.

But how will you know when the sun rises (or sets) if it does this when you are asleep? Most daily newspapers publish the hours of the sunrise and sunset.

Use your chart to track the daily (or weekly or monthly) changes of the sunrise and sunset. What does this tell you about the length of day and night from one month to another?

August

Day:	Sunrise (AM):	Sunset (PM):	Sky Conditions:
1	4:36	7:04	Cloudy
2	4:37	7:03	Sunny
3	4:38	7:02	Sunny
4	4:39	7:00	Cloudy
5	4:40	6:59	Cloudy
6	4:42	6:58	Rainy
7	4:43	6:57	Rainy
8	4:44	6:55	Sunny
9	4:45	6:54	Sunny
10	4:46	6:53	Sunny

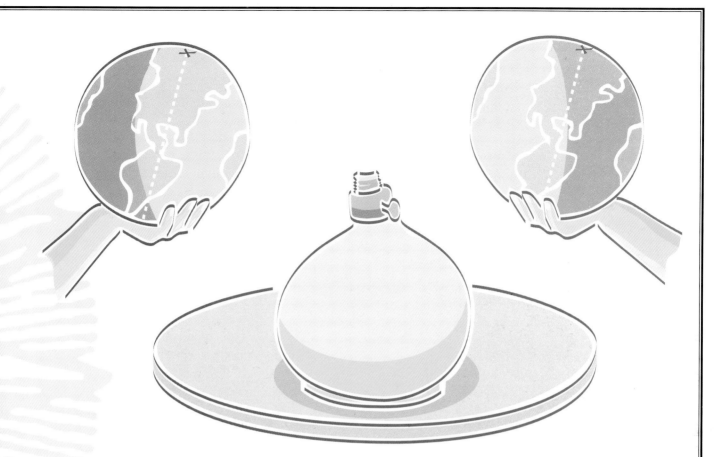

THE REASONS FOR THE SEASONS

The four seasons of the year are reversed in Australia (and other countries that lie below the Equator). That means when it's summer in North America, it's winter in Australia.

Why is this? It's all because of the way the earth is tilted. As the earth moves around the sun in its yearly cycle of 365 days, one pole or the other is pointed more toward the sun.

You can demonstrate this with a globe (or a balloon that has the continents drawn on it) and a lamp without its shade. Place the lamp on a table in the middle of the room. Holding the globe so that it is tilted, slowly walk around the lamp table.

Notice which part of the earth gets the most sun (the most light from the lamp) when it's winter in North America. It's that part of the globe below the Equator where Australia is located, isn't it?

PICTURE THIS

"Lighting the Way" was not only a myth the Aborigines told, it was also one they illustrated in their art.

Beautiful paintings done on tree bark have been made by the tribespeople of northern Australia for centuries. Once meant to illustrate the myths for the men and boys of the tribe, today these paintings are admired all over the world.

The bark for the paintings comes from the stringybark eucalyptus tree and is stripped from the trees once the wet season has begun. Curved sheets of the bark are heated over a fire and gradually straightened. The sheets are then laid flat on the ground, weighted with rocks, and allowed to cool.

Natural pigments are used to make the paint. Only four colors are used in the paintings—black (or dark brown), used for the backgrounds and to fill in the main figures; white, used to outline the main figures; a rusty red; and a soft, earthen yellow.

Most traditional Aboriginal pictures have no top or bottom. They are meant to be viewed from any side. Why? This goes back to the days when groups of men or boys crouched around a painting on the ground, and it was important that all could see it clearly.

Try your hand at painting in the style of the Arnhem Land artists, using a grocery bag instead of bark. Illustrate something from the story or base your design on a favorite Australian bird or animal, such as the emu, the koala, or the kangaroo. While you can paint your design, you'll find it easier to do detailed work with crayons.

○ **Brown paper grocery bag**
○ **Pencil**
○ **Crayons in brown or black, white, red, and yellow**

1 Tear off the bottom of the grocery bag and rip it along the seam to open it up. Carefully tear the bag into a rectangle.

2 Lightly sketch your design on the paper in pencil. Use the example shown here, or come up with your own idea.

3 Outline the main figure or figures in white. In traditional paintings, figures that are meant to appear close by are shown larger than those meant to appear in the distance. Gods and spirits are also shown larger, to emphasize their importance.

4 Fill in the figures with a solid color, like black, to make them stand out. Decorate parts of the background with closely spaced dots and dashes, using the red and yellow paint.

STAR LIGHT, STAR BRIGHT

Like many peoples around the world, the Aborigines told many tales about the sky and what they saw there. They invented stories that explained the daily movement of the sun and the different phases of the moon. And, of course, the appearance of the morning star.

Today, we know that the "morning star" is not a star at all. It is actually the planet Venus, visible not only in the morning, but in the early evening, too.

Still, many people refer to Venus as the morning, or evening, star, because it looks like a bright star. In fact, apart from the sun and the moon, Venus is the brightest object in the sky. It does not create its own light but reflects the light from the sun, just as the moon does. And like the moon, Venus has different *phases* (when different parts of the planet are lit and when it is not visible at all).

Some morning, when the sky is just beginning to lighten, face east and see if you can spot Venus, quite close to the horizon. Facing west, do the same in the evening once the sun has gone down. When the planet is in its "full" phase, you can easily spot it with the naked eye. Other phases are easier to see with binoculars or a telescope.

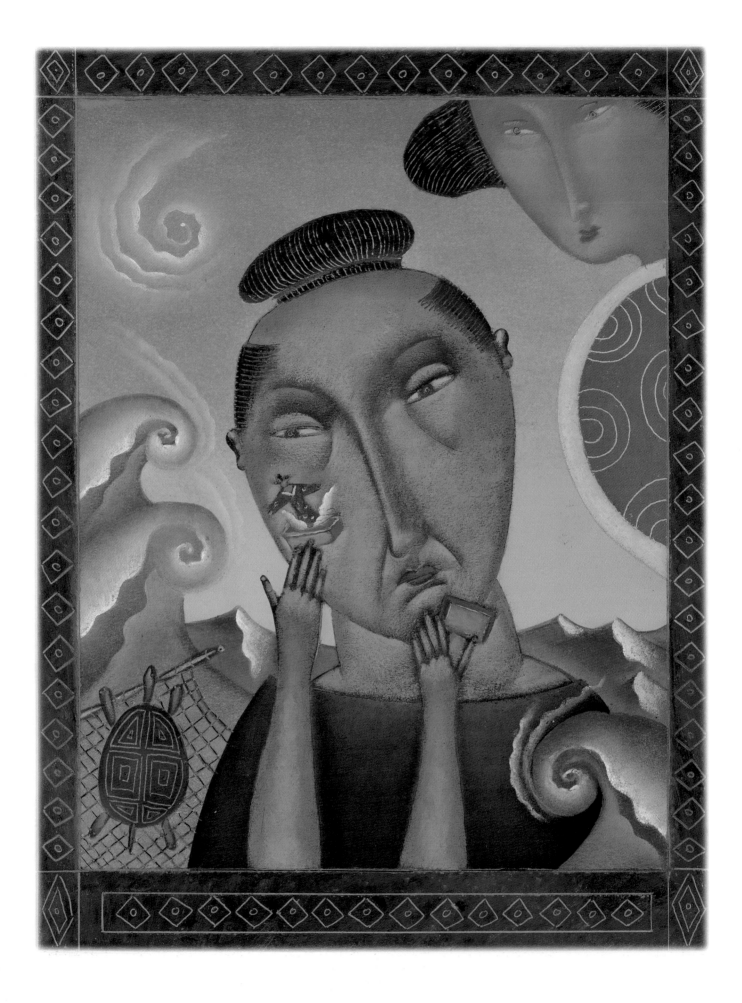

✠

Ignoring the instructions or well-meaning advice of others is a popular theme in many tales around the world. Often a story's hero is able to overcome any resulting problems and everything turns out all right. Not so in this Japanese tale, which ends on a more somber note.

Urashima the Fisherman

any years ago in a small village in the Tango province, there lived an old man and his wife and their grown son Urashima (oo-RAH-she-mah).

Each day Urashima would row out to sea in a small boat. There he would drop his nets in the water and pull up the fish that got trapped in them. When luck was with him, Urashima might pull up several huge baskets of fish, which his mother and father would then sell at the village market. This was how they lived.

One day, Urashima rowed out to sea as usual. When he pulled up his nets, he hadn't caught a single fish. He tried again, and again his nets were completely empty.

Urashima had no luck the next day, nor the next. He was ready to go home empty-handed once again when he dropped the nets into the water one last time. When he pulled them up, he found he had snared a sea turtle.

Urashima carefully untangled the netting from around the turtle's flippers. He turned around to free a bit of the rope that was caught on the prow of his boat. When Urashima turned back, he saw that the turtle had changed into a beautiful young woman, dressed in a shimmering kimono patterned with a design of clouds.

"I've been watching you for a long time," the young woman said to Urashima. "I so wanted to meet you."

"Who are you?" asked Urashima. He stared uncertainly at the mysterious woman.

"I am not from your world," the woman replied. "I am an Immortal, and I live in the sky. Yes, it's true," she added, seeing the disbelief in Urashima's eyes. "I am a goddess."

Urashima nodded his understanding and somehow accepted that a mere mortal such as himself could see and talk to a god. Then he asked, "But why did you wish to talk with me?"

"I have loved you from the first moment I set eyes on you," the woman said. "I want to bring you to my home. Will you come with me?"

Urashima suddenly lost all his fear, and replied, "Yes, I will come with you. But how shall we get to your home?"

"Take the oars in your hands and shut your eyes," the woman said.

Only a few seconds passed before the sky goddess told Urashima to open his eyes. He saw they were nearing a large island with earth the color of jade. He could see a magnificent palace with watchtowers that rose even higher than the clouds. It was unlike anything Urashima had ever seen, or even imagined.

The two landed on a pebbly beach and strolled hand in hand up to the gates of the palace. "My parents are most anxious to meet you," the goddess said. Urashima was introduced to her mother and father, and they greeted him warmly, telling him how gladdened they were by this rare meeting of gods and mortals.

That evening, Urashima was invited to join the family at a special banquet held in his honor. The food was delicious and beautifully prepared. After the meal, Urashima and the Immortals talked of the future.

"When the sun goes down," the goddess's father said, "you shall be man and wife." And so they were wed, and Urashima lived happily with his new wife and her family in their home in the sky.

All was fine for three years—three years that went by so quickly it seemed like only three days. Then one day Urashima felt a pang of longing for his own mother and father and for his life as a fisherman in their village. Each day he felt the tug of his past more strongly, until he finally spoke to his wife about it.

"My parents must be very worried about me," Urashima told his wife. "I never told them where I was going. Besides, I miss them greatly, and I wish I could see them and make sure they are all right."

"I understand," Urashima's wife said kindly. "But when we wed, we promised we would be as true to one another as the rocks are to the mountains. Your parents are fine; I know they are. Your home-sickness will go away, too, I am sure."

But Urashima missed his own family more and more, and finally he persuaded his wife and her parents that he must be allowed to return to his village. They were saddened to see him go, but they told Urashima he could return to the kingdom of the clouds any time he chose.

"Take this box," said Urashima's wife, handing him a tiny box that fit in the palm of his hand. "Just grip it tightly in your hand when you wish to come back to us. But you must *never* open the box . . . *ever*," she warned, kissing her husband good-bye.

Urashima got into his boat, and his father-in-law told him to close his eyes. A few seconds later the boat ground to a gentle halt. Urashima opened his eyes and saw he was back in his village. But it looked so different he could hardly recognize it.

Urashima walked toward where his house should have been, but he could find it nowhere. He stopped a woman on the street. "Excuse me," he said, "but could you tell me where I might find the family of Urashima the fisherman?"

"Who?" replied the old woman. "Urashima? Never heard of him."

"But he lived with his mother and father in a house right on this spot," insisted Urashima.

"Oh, yes," the old woman recalled. "I know who you are talking about now. I remember my great-grandfather telling a story about a fellow named Urashima. They say he went out fishing in his boat one day and never returned. But that was over three hundred years ago."

Urashima was speechless for a moment. "I don't understand," he stammered.

"Well, I don't understand why you're looking for someone who has been missing for three hundred years," replied the old woman. She walked away, shaking her head.

Urashima strode from one end of the village to the other, searching for at least something that he might recognize. Had all traces of his mother and father disappeared? Could it be that three years in the kingdom in the clouds were really three hundred years on earth? He looked down at the box he held in his hand. "Perhaps this box holds the answers," he thought to himself.

Ignoring his wife's stern warning, Urashima lifted its lid. A white cloud rose from the box and Urashima could just make out the shape of the goddess as it floated up into the sky and vanished from view.

"What have I done!" Urashima wailed, realizing that he would never see his wife again. He sat on the ground and held his head in his hands and wept.

When Urashima had dried his tears, he sang of his love for his wife. "My love," he sang, "each morning when I wake, I will listen for the sound of the waves breaking against the shore of your island home."

If only Urashima hadn't opened the box, the villagers said from that day on, he could have returned to his beloved wife.

"If only," Urashima sang, "if only."

URASHIMA THE FISHERMAN

COUNTRY: **Japan**
CONTINENT: **Asia**
LANGUAGE: **Japanese**
CAPITAL: **Tokyo**
FLAG:

READ ALL ABOUT IT!

Most of the tales in this book are very old. They have been handed down from one generation to the next, by storytellers sitting around fires, inside igloos, and at children's bedsides.

Many of those storytellers knew the tales from memory, and they probably changed the stories slightly each time they told them. But some storytellers may have read the tales from books, just as you are reading them today. Did you know that people have been collecting tales in books for hundreds and hundreds of years?

"Urashima the Fisherman" is an example of a tale that was written down long ago. It was found in a book that was published in the year 713 A.D. That year, the different provinces of Japan were asked to note something of their history and special features, and this tale from Tango Province was written down at that time.

Can you figure out just how long ago that was? That's right—just subtract 713 from the current year. Wow, that was a long time ago!

713 A.D.

YOU'LL NEED

○ **2 sheets of heavy paper, 8 ½ inches by 11 inches (21.5 cm by 28 cm)**
○ **Pencil**
○ **Scissors**
○ **White glue**
○ **Crayons, markers, or paint**

LONG LIVE THE TURTLE!

When the sky goddess first met Urashima, she appeared as a sea turtle. In Japanese lore, the sea turtle is considered a magical creature and a symbol of *immortality*, or living forever. Turtles symbolize long life in many cultures, no doubt because turtles live a long time themselves.

This year, honor your grandparents—and their long lives— with turtle birthday cards. The pop-up design is sure to delight them just as much as the special written message.

Cut ——
Fold -----

1 Fold both sheets of paper in half along the long edge. Draw a half-turtle design on the folded edge of one of the papers. Cut along the solid lines only (the dotted line is a fold line).

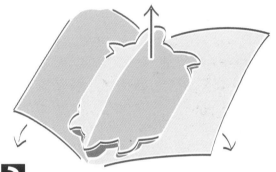

2 Open the paper and push the turtle shape toward you, refolding the turtle's center fold, and folding along the dotted lines so that the turtle shape pops up as shown.

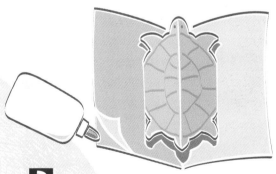

3 Glue this paper to the other folded sheet, making sure not to get any glue on the pop-up portion. Decorate the front and the inside of the card.

BOUND AND TIED

You can bind your own folktale in book form using this ingenious accordion-fold method from Asia. Accordion-folded books were often used for poetry and artwork.

The instructions here are for a teeny, tiny book only 3 ¼ inches (8.3 cm) in size, but you can adapt this method to make a book any size you like. You can also make the book longer by lengthening the folded strip. How? By folding two (or more) strips, and joining them with a small overlap.

```
YOU'LL NEED
```
○ **Strip of thin paper, 3 inches by 24 inches (7.5 cm by 60 cm)**
○ **2 pieces of poster board, 3 ¼ inches (8.3 cm) square**
○ **Ruler**
○ **White glue**
○ **Fabric ribbon, ¼-inch (5 mm) wide and 24 inches (60 cm) long**
○ **Pen and markers, or crayons**

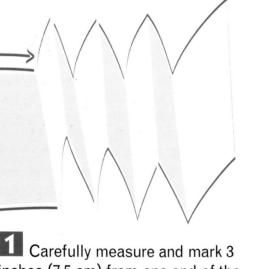

3"

3"

3"

1 Carefully measure and mark 3 inches (7.5 cm) from one end of the paper strip. Fold the paper at that mark, creasing it well. Continue folding the paper, back and forth accordion-style, until you reach the end. You will have folded it seven times, making eight square "pages."

2 Measure and mark a square on one of the poster board squares, ¼-inch (5 mm) from each edge. Carefully smear some glue on the poster board, taking care to stay inside the lines.

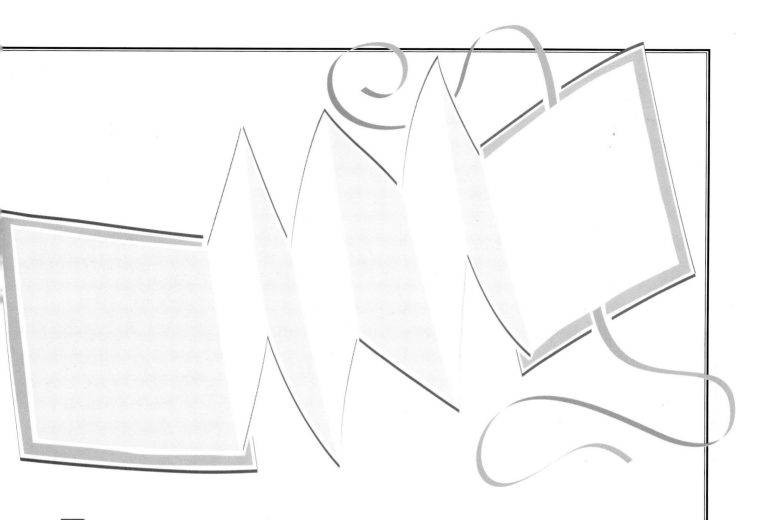

3 Lay the middle of the ribbon in the center of the glued square. Then place one end of the folded paper strip over the ribbon, using the drawn lines to help you position it. Mark the other poster board square, then glue the other end of the folded paper strip to it. Place the accordion-fold book under a weight, such as a heavy book, and let dry.

Write and illustrate your tale on the "pages," front and back. Decorate the cover any way you like. To hold the book closed, tie the ribbons at both sides.

NOTEWORTHY

The song Urashima sang at the end of the story was sad, certainly, but it would have sounded sad to us even if we didn't know what the words in Japanese meant. Why? Because traditional Japanese music uses a scale of notes very different from the one we are used to hearing.

The different notes give Japanese music a mysterious, mournful sound, somewhat like the melodies you make when you play just the black keys of a piano. Try plunking out a simple melody on the piano like this. What does it sound like to you?

PAPER PEOPLE

Origami, the ancient Japanese art of paper-folding, is known and loved all over the world today. No wonder, when you think how a sheet of paper can be transformed into hundreds of different shapes, simply by folding it!

Whether you're new to origami or not, you're sure to be charmed by this model of a squat figure dressed in a kimono, or robe. It is thought to be one of the oldest origami designs. The figure represents Yakko-san (yah-koh-SAHN), a traditional Japanese clown. It's a simple design, but there's a hidden surprise. Lift the edges of Yakko-san's kimono sleeves to find two tiny, pointed hands!

Fold several Yakko-san figures to stand for the characters in "Urashima the Fisherman." Using white paper, you can first fold the figures, then color in the kimonos (drawing clouds on the sky goddess's robe, for example) and draw simple features on the faces.

The key to successful paper-folding is taking the time to make each fold accurately and to crease the folds well. Happy folding!

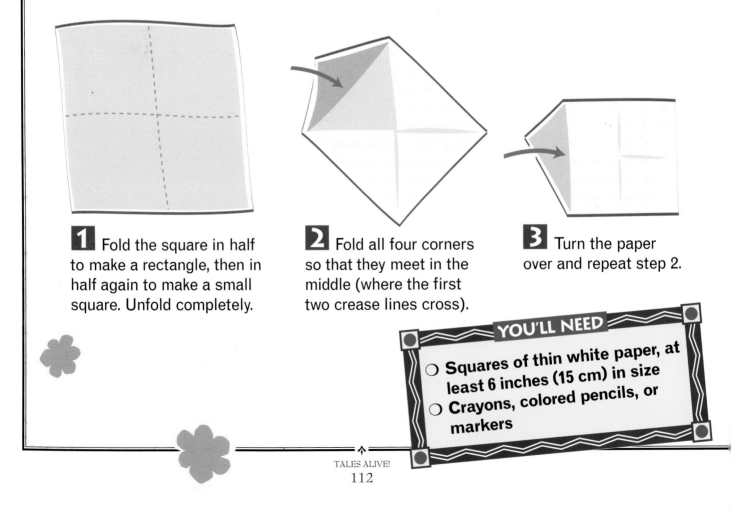

1 Fold the square in half to make a rectangle, then in half again to make a small square. Unfold completely.

2 Fold all four corners so that they meet in the middle (where the first two crease lines cross).

3 Turn the paper over and repeat step 2.

YOU'LL NEED

○ Squares of thin white paper, at least 6 inches (15 cm) in size
○ Crayons, colored pencils, or markers

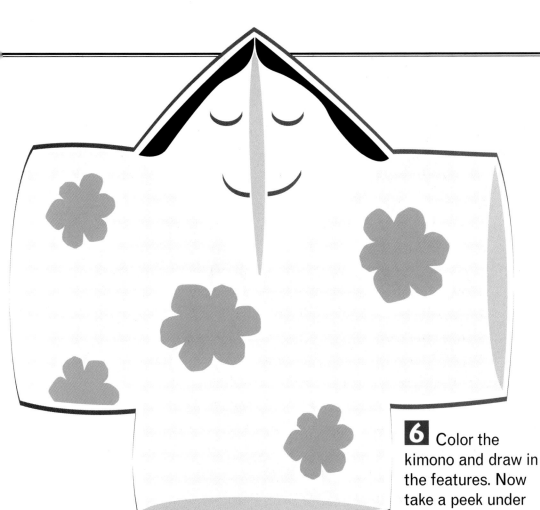

6 Color the kimono and draw in the features. Now take a peek under the kimono sleeves!

HANG IT ALL!

Here's an idea: Make a mobile with your origami figures. Tie a length of string to the middle of a thin stick such as a bamboo skewer. Tie a shorter stick near one end of the first stick. Attach string to all of the origami figures and then tie the figures to the sticks, moving them, as necessary, to balance the mobile.

4 Turn the paper over and repeat step 2 once again.

5 Turn the paper over. Insert your finger between the raw edges of one of the corner squares. Push the point away from the center, flattening the square, as shown in the diagram. Do the same with two of the other corners.

See how those flattened parts look like two straight sleeves and the bottom hem of a kimono? The diamond shape at the top is the head.

This story has several classic elements found in many tales. First, there's the powerful ruler who's in search of a suitable husband for his daughter. Then there's the young man who triumphs despite what others think of him. Last but not least, there's a happy-ever-after ending.

The Most Wonderful Gift

ong, long ago there lived a mighty sultan who loved his only daughter dearly. When the time came for her to marry, the sultan began to search for a suitable husband. How would he choose just one from among the many eligible princes of neighboring kingdoms? The sultan thought this over, then decided to send out a proclamation that read, "The prince who brings me the most wonderful gift in the world shall have my daughter's hand in marriage."

You can just imagine the rare and precious gifts the anxious young princes brought before the mighty sultan. There were rainbow-colored pearls from the deepest ocean beds that brought rain when tossed into the air. There were trees that bore pomegranates with seeds of purest gold, and birds in cages whose songs were guaranteed to banish sadness. The sultan thanked the princes for their gifts, but none of the gifts stood out above the rest.

It so happened that in a land far away there lived three princes—

brothers, in fact—who were all of marrying age. When they learned of the sultan's search for a worthy husband, they decided to set out together to find suitable gifts. They walked from their home to the bazaar, or marketplace, each carrying a sack filled with gold.

The eldest brother wasted no time choosing a gift. He was intrigued by a small mirror in which a person could see what was happening anywhere in the world.

"This is truly a special gift," thought the prince, and handed over his sack of gold in exchange for the looking glass.

The second brother, a rather adventurous young man, stopped to admire a beautifully woven carpet. This was no ordinary rug, however. It was a magic carpet on which a person could fly any distance in the twinkling of an eye. "Surely there is no finer gift," declared the second prince, paying for the carpet with his sack of gold.

The youngest brother had a more difficult time making up his mind. Had it not been for the lemon seller singing "Wonderful lemons! Lemons for sale!" the youngest prince might have left the bazaar empty-handed. "What makes these lemons so wonderful?" he asked the merchant.

"Ah, the juice from one of these lemons will cure any illness there is," the merchant replied. The prince considered this for a moment, then bought one of the lemons.

The two older brothers scoffed at the youngest prince when they saw he had purchased a mere lemon—and for a whole sack of gold!

They had always suspected their kindhearted brother wasn't that smart. But there wasn't much time to tease him, for at that moment the eldest brother was showing off his mirror, and what should they see in its glass but the sultan's daughter, lying deathly pale in her bed.

"Quickly!" commanded the second brother. "Let us travel there at once!" The three brothers climbed onto the flying carpet, and before they knew it they found themselves at the sultan's palace. They were met by the sultan, who had tears in his eyes. "Please go away," he begged. "My daughter, the princess, is gravely ill."

The youngest brother stepped forward and spoke. "Sire," he said, bowing low, "please accept this lemon. Its juice will cure your daughter of whatever ails her."

Well, by now you've probably guessed that indeed the princess was cured by this magical lemon. The sultan was delighted and thanked the brothers. Only then did he ask, "But what brings you three here today?"

The eldest brother spoke first. "We have come to ask for your daughter's hand in marriage. Each of us has brought a gift. May I show you mine?" He handed the mirror to the sultan, explaining, "This is the mirror in which we saw that the princess was ill, your Majesty. Not only that, with this mirror you will be able to keep an eye on your entire kingdom. I think you will agree it is a most worthy gift."

"Ah, yes," admitted the sultan, "your mirror played a most important role in saving my beloved daughter. And it would make my job as ruler a good deal simpler."

"But," interrupted the second brother, "were it not for my gift, the flying carpet, we would not have been able to travel here so swiftly. This same carpet will take you anywhere you choose to go, in less time than it takes you to snap your fingers. I believe there is not a better gift than my own."

"True, my daughter was very close to death, and your speedy arrival saved her," said the sultan. "This carpet would prove very useful for traveling about my vast domain." Turning to the youngest prince, he asked, "And what gift have you brought?"

The youngest prince held up what was left of the lemon. "This lemon was my gift," he replied.

The other brothers began to laugh, and the sultan himself could not help from smiling. It was at that moment that the princess spoke. "The mirror and the carpet are certainly fine gifts," she began, "and I am grateful for the roles they played today. But it was the lemon that restored my life, and surely life is the most wonderful gift of all."

"Quite right you are!" exclaimed the sultan, hugging first his daughter and then the youngest prince. "Your gift is the greatest by far, and I am pleased to offer you my daughter's hand in marriage, with my blessing."

And so the youngest prince and the princess were married. Theirs was a truly magnificent wedding, followed by a long and happy marriage. May we all be so lucky!

WHERE IN THE WORLD IS TURKEY?

COUNTRY:	**Turkey**
CONTINENT:	**Asia**
LANGUAGE:	**Turkish**
CAPITAL:	**Ankara**
FLAG:	

YOU FIGURE IT OUT

A similar version of this tale is told in Togo, a small country in West Africa. In the African tale, the three brothers are transported not by carpet but by a pair of magic sandals. Other little details make the story more "African." But there is another interesting difference. In the Togo tale, the ending is not revealed. Instead, the listeners are asked to decide which they think is the most wonderful gift.

Tales with such endings are popular in Africa. These kinds of stories are more than entertainment; they are even more than a way to get across a message. They are a way of getting a group of people to discuss important issues.

You can use this Turkish tale to do the same. You know how it ends, but you can have your parents or your friends read it—all except for the ending. Ask them to choose which gift they think is the most wonderful. Which do they select, and why do they say they chose that particular one?

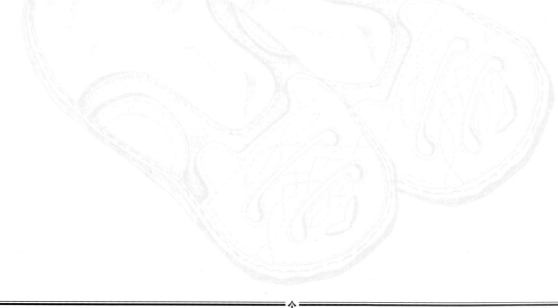

MIRROR, MIRROR

Mirrors figure in lots of tales from around the world. And, like the mirror in this story, they don't always reflect what is placed in front of them. Just think how the mirror in *Snow White* showed the wicked stepmother who was the fairest in the land.

You can make a special hanging mirror of your own, decorated with traditional Turkish designs. Now when you look into this mirror you'll see . . . well, just wait and see!

1 Smear petroleum jelly on one side of the plate. Using the papier-mâché paste, paste at least eight layers of newspaper strips on this side of the plate.

Let the strips extend over the plate's edge; they will be trimmed later. Place the plate in a warm spot for several days until completely dry.

- Plastic or heavy paper plate
- Petroleum jelly
- Newspaper, torn into 1-inch (2.5 cm) strips
- Papier-mâché paste, made from 4 cups (500 g) flour mixed with 4 cups (1 l) water until smooth
- Sandpaper
- Acrylic paints
- Paintbrush
- Awl or other sharp tool
- Thick cotton string
- Round pocket mirror
- Household cement

2 Pry the papier-mâché away from the plate. Trim the edges with scissors, then sand any rough spots. Paint both the front and back with a light-colored base coat (you may need two coats for complete coverage). On the side that will show (choose either side), draw your designs in pencil. Remember, the mirror will be glued in the very center. Paint the designs and let dry.

3 Have an adult help you poke two holes for the string. Cut a piece of string 12 inches (30 cm) long, and thread it through the two holes. Knot the ends of the string. An adult should also glue the mirror in place, as household cement is a very strong glue. When the glue has set, hang the mirror and take a peek!

LAST, BUT NOT LEAST

The number three figures in many tales, often for different reasons (for more on the number three, see page 31). Sometimes there are three characters in the story who are competing with one another. Just as in "The Most Wonderful Gift," the third person of the group is often considered too young, lazy, or dull-witted to have even the slightest chance of ever "winning."

Can you think of any characters in other tales that fit this description? How about Cinderella, whose two stepsisters cannot possibly imagine her foot fitting into the glass slipper?

A funny thing happens to the supposedly weakest characters in these tales. They triumph, in spite of what others think of them!

Sometimes these characters are simply misunderstood, and when they are given the chance they prove that they are perfectly able. But, just as often, these characters "win" by showing that they are the most considerate or the most caring of the three.

This is what happens to the youngest brother in "The Most Wonderful Gift." His choice of the healing lemon proves that he has a wonderful gift of his own—kindness and compassion.

Up, Up and Away

Wouldn't you love to have your own magic carpet? Just imagine—you and your friends could play chase high above the clouds, and you'd even get to sleep later on school days because getting to school would be a snap!

Well, no promises that this carpet will hover over the floor (unless you choose to hang it on a wall!), but gazing at it may transport your thoughts to faraway places.

YOU'LL NEED

- ○ **Small woven cotton rug or bath mat**
- ○ **Fabric paints (in squeeze bottles and jars)**
- ○ **Paintbrush**

1 Plan your designs on a separate piece of paper, or decorate the rug as you go. You'll find it's easy to "draw" lines with the paint that comes in squeeze bottles; shapes drawn this way can be filled in with a solid color using a brush. You won't get complete paint coverage if you are painting a bath mat, because the terry loops are bumpy. Diluting the paints a bit may help.

2 Have an adult help you heat-set the paint according to the paint manufacturer's recommendation. Then you're ready for takeoff!

Did you know the humble lemon does have healing powers? Lemons are full of vitamin C, which is important for building healthy cells, as well as for helping other nutrients get absorbed by the body.

Lemons are also valued for their taste. If you've ever bitten into a lemon, you know we're not talking about eating lemons that way, but just think what a squeeze of lemon does for fish and other seafood. And can you imagine lemon meringue pie without the lemons?

Lemons are used a lot in Turkish cookery and are found in everything from soup to candy. Lemons also find their way into all sorts of drinks, including this "magic" lemonade!

Magic Potion

FOOD FOR THOUGHT
TALES ALIVE! RECIPE

YOU'LL NEED

- ○ 4 lemons
- ○ 4 cups (1 l) cold water
- ○ ½ cup (125 g) sugar
- ○ 1 tablespoon (15 ml) rose water*

* Rose water can be found in Middle Eastern and Turkish markets, as well as in the gourmet section of many supermarkets.

Roll the lemons on a hard surface, such as a countertop, to soften them up. You'll get a lot more juice from them that way. Cut each lemon in half and squeeze all the juice into a pitcher. Add the water, sugar, and rose water, stirring until the sugar is completely dissolved. Pour into tall glasses filled with ice cubes.

Serves 4.

Other Books You Will Enjoy

f you liked the tales in this book, you'll enjoy reading other folk literature from around the world. In addition to the following anthologies of tales, many individual tales from around the world have been illustrated and published in book form. Look for these, and other titles, in your local library and bookstores.

Abrahams, Roger D. *African Folktales.* New York: Pantheon Books, 1983.

Afanasev, Aleksandr. *Russian Fairy Tales.* New York: Pantheon Books, 1976.

Allen, Louis A. *Time Before Morning: Art and Myth of the Australian Aborigines.* New York: Thomas Y. Crowell, 1975.

Bruchac, Joseph. *Native American Stories.* Golden: Fulcrum Publishing, 1991.

Calvino, Italo. *Italian Folktales.* New York: Harcourt Brace Jovanovich, 1980.

Ellis, Jean A. *From the Dreamtime: Australian Aboriginal Legends.* New York: Collins Dove, 1991.

Fairman, Tony. *Bury My Bones but Keep My Words: African Tales for Retelling.* New York: Henry Holt and Company, 1992.

Finger, Charles J. *Tales from Silver Lands.* New York: Doubleday & Company, 1924.

Hamilton, Virginia. *In the Beginning: Creation Stories from Around the World.* San Diego: Harcourt Brace Jovanovich, 1988.

Hanh, Thich Nhat. *A Taste of Earth and Other Legends of Vietnam*. Berkeley: Parallax Press, 1993.

Haviland, Virginia. *Favorite Fairy Tales Told in India*. Boston: Little, Brown and Company, 1973.

Jones, Gwyn. *Scandinavian Legends and Folk-tales*. Oxford: Oxford University Press, 1956, 1972.

Kelsey, Alice Geer. *Once the Hodja*. New York: David McKay Company, 1943.

Leodhas, Sorche Nic. *Thistle & Thyme: Tales and Legends from Scotland*. New York: Holt, Rinehart and Winston, 1962.

Melzack, Ronald. *The Day Tuk Became a Hunter and Other Stories*. New York: Dodd, Mead & Company, 1968.

Norman, Howard, selector and editor. *Northern Tales: Traditional Stories of Eskimo and Indian Peoples*. New York: Pantheon Books, 1990.

Opie, Iona and Peter. *The Classic Fairy Tales*. London: Book Club Associates, 1974.

Ramanujan, A.K. *Folktales from India*. New York: Pantheon Books, 1991.

Shah, Indries. *World Tales*. New York: Harcourt Brace Jovanovich, 1979.

Thompson, Stith. *One Hundred Favorite Folktales*. Bloomington: University of Indiana Press, 1986.

Tyler, Royall, editor and translator. *Japanese Tales*. New York: Pantheon Books, 1987.

Vittorini, Domenico. *Old Italian Tales*. New York: David McCay, 1958.

Walker, Barbara K. *A Treasury of Turkish Folktales for Children*. Hamden, Conn.: Linnet Books, 1988.

Williamson, Duncan. *Tales of the Seal People: Scottish Folk Tales*. Brooklyn: Interlink Books, 1992.

Yolen, Jane, editor. *Favorite Folktales from Around the World*. New York: Pantheon Books, 1986.

Zipes, Jack, translator. *The Complete Fairy Tales of the Brothers Grimm*. New York: Bantam Books, 1992.

Index

To Activity Sections